THE HOUSE OF COMMONS
COOKERY BOOK

Over 150 Favourite Recipes Contributed by

Members of Parliament

Compiled by
Charles Irving, MP

Foreword by
The Right Honourable Bernard Weatherill, MP,
Speaker of The House of Commons

Illustrated by
Paul Cox

CENTURY
London   Melbourne   Auckland   Johannesburg

First published in 1987 by Century Hutchinson Ltd,
Brookmount House, 62–65 Chandos Place, Covent Garden,
London WC2N 4NW

Century Hutchinson Australia Pty Ltd,
PO Box 496, 16–22 Church Street, Hawthorn, Victoria 3122,
Australia

Century Hutchinson New Zealand Ltd,
PO Box 40–086, Glenfield, Auckland 10,
New Zealand

Century Hutchinson South Africa Pty Ltd,
PO Box 337, Bergvlei, 2012 South Africa

British Library Cataloguing in Publication Data

Irving, Charles
    The House of Commons cookery book : 150
    favourite recipes contributed by Members of
    Parliament.
    1. Cookery, International
    I. Title
    641.5   TX725.A1

ISBN 0–7126–1813–9
Edited by Susan Fleming
Designed by Dave Goodman

Set in Linotron Bembo by
Deltatype, Ellesmere Port, Cheshire
Printed and bound in Great Britain by
Butler & Tanner Ltd, Frome, Somerset

Note:
In the course of the production of this book there have been a number of changes of Members' positions in the Houses of Parliament. While every effort has been made to keep up with these changes, it has, inevitably, not been possible to make all the necessary alterations.

Contents

FOREWORD

I am delighted to be associated with this enterprise – a book of House of Commons recipes compiled by Charles Irving, MP for Cheltenham, the royalties from which will go to ChildLine and other charities.

All those who work in and around Westminster – Members, staff and journalists in the Press Gallery – have contributed enthusiastically, revealing a wide-ranging interest in food, from simple and wholesome local fare associated with particular parts of the country, to sophisticated international dishes. Themes which recur in the recipes are thrift, advance preparation, speed of preparation and keeping qualities – all clues to the lifestyle of the contributors – as well as occasional apologia for recipes which are not guaranteed to make those that partake of them lose weight!

It is a delightful, delicious and entertaining collection of recipes, and I should like to thank all those who have given their time and effort (including, I suspect, many wives, mothers and daughters of the less culinary-minded male Members) in aid of such a worthy cause.

The Right Honourable Bernard Weatherill, MP
SPEAKER OF THE HOUSE OF COMMONS

INTRODUCTION

Few people realize in the House of Commons up to 10,000 people a day are fed. These include 650 members – half of whom, on average, use the facilities every day – their assistants, secretaries, journalists from the Press Gallery, Officers, visitors, and the staff of the House of Commons itself. No small number to keep happy – and I do not exaggerate!

The Refreshment Department of the House of Commons – under the capable control of John Smillie, the General Manager – caters for this demand in no fewer than twenty-five catering outlets, which number among them the Members' and Strangers' Dining Rooms, the Harcourt Grill Room (where Ieuan Jones, our famous harpist, plays regularly in the evenings), the Press Gallery Restaurant, various cafeterias and a number of private dining rooms – for which demand is so great that virtually six months' notice in advance is required for booking! We also have a total of nine bars. The department deals weekly with some seventy special luncheons or banquets, as well as having the privilege of providing for all State occasions in the State Apartments of Speaker's House.

It is thus a great responsibility being Chairman of the famous (or infamous?) Committee, which position I have held since 1979 with the splendid support of colleagues from all parties who serve with me. We have achieved some considerable profitability and, to stimulate that, we now serve luncheons on the Terrace offering a delightful buffet, afternoon teas for constituency parties, receptions and cocktail parties in the evening for 300 to 400 guests. We are at the moment eagerly anticipating the opening of the new Bridge Street site where we shall have additional catering facilities for over 1,000 people. This will enable us to extend the arrangements of the Palace to provide light refreshments – which we cannot at present – for constituents visiting MPs (they travel long distances and are unable to obtain even a cup of tea). I hope I shall have the opportunity of seeing that establishment opened and being well-run – a modest ambition!

It seemed a logical next step to put together a book which would be representative of the House and all those that work there, something that would benefit not only those that bought it – for the recipes display a superb variety – but also those less fortunate. For this reason, I dedicated the proceeds to charitable causes, but with priority to the ChildLine Appeal. May you enjoy the contributions from all of us in the House – and my thanks to all colleagues and friends who have made the book possible.

Charles Irving, MP
CHAIRMAN, CATERING SUB-COMMITTEE

Soups
and
Starters

Sir David Price, DL, MP
— MEMBER OF PARLIAMENT FOR EASTLEIGH —

GARLIC SOUP

There are many variations of garlic soup, known as *soupe à l'ail* by the French. I have my own variation of a classic recipe for garlic soup, based on a recipe of Elizabeth David's, an inspiration to all cooks of my generation. This is a soup which I especially recommend to those who like their garlic straight!

This is a very suitable starter to a summer lunch in the garden. It should be followed by cold meats, especially good smoked ham and smoked chicken, and accompanied with a garlicky dressing.

I recommend washing it down with either a strong dry draught Somerset or Normandy cider, or a robust red wine. I suggest the 'black wine' Cahors from south-west France, a plummy Barbera from Piedmont, or an Alicanti Bouschet from California.

To round off this garden lunch, I recommend a blue cheese, either Blue Cheshire or Gorgonzola, with warmed brown wholemeal bread.

SERVES ABOUT 10
5 tablespoons olive oil
24 garlic cloves, peeled
1.8 litres (3 pints) warmed chicken stock
salt and freshly ground black pepper
a pinch each of grated nutmeg and ground mace
3 standard egg yolks
GARNISH
fried bread croûtons

Put 2 tablespoons of the olive oil into a deep stew pan, and heat gently. In this oil melt gently the cloves of garlic without letting them actually get brown.

Pour in the warmed chicken stock, and season with salt, pepper, nutmeg and mace – which is particularly important. Cook for 15 minutes. Put the soup through a sieve, and return to the pan to heat through.

In a bowl beat up the egg yolks with the remaining olive oil. Stir some of the soup into the eggs, then pour the egg mixture back into the soup without letting it boil again.

Serve garnished with the fried croûtons.

———————————— ○ ————————————

Humfrey Malins, MP
— MEMBER OF PARLIAMENT FOR CROYDON NORTH WEST —

LEEK (OR CELERY) SOUP

Since I have given up rugby, cooking is my main way of relaxing. I love making soups. My speciality, and very simple, is leek (or celery) soup.

The word leak makes a politician nervous. But making a delicious leek soup takes my mind right off politics – how healthy in all respects!

SERVES 4–6
25 g (1 oz) butter
1 large potato, peeled and chopped
1 large onion, peeled and chopped
3 large leeks (or 1 whole head celery), trimmed and chopped
900 ml (1½ pints) chicken stock (can be made with a cube)
grated cheese

Melt the butter in a pan and add the potato, onion and leeks (or celery). Use the whites of the leeks plus a little of the green (and add the leafy bits of the celery). Let cook gently for a few minutes and then add the stock. Simmer for 40 minutes and then put it all through a blender. Stir in the grated cheese or sprinkle into individual bowls.

———————————— ○ ————————————

Dr Jeremy Bray, MP
— MEMBER OF PARLIAMENT FOR MOTHERWELL SOUTH —

MEDITERRANEAN FISH SOUP

A cross between a soup and a stew, with an unexpected combination of flavours. A complete meal if served with hot garlic bread.

Per person
1 small to medium potato, peeled and thinly sliced
100 g (¼ lb) firm white fish (monkfish for special occasions)
1 carrot, scrubbed and thinly sliced
1 celery stick, trimmed and thinly sliced
juice of 1–2 oranges
1 teaspoon grated orange rind
½ garlic clove, peeled and chopped
sufficient water or fish stock to cover
freshly ground black pepper
To serve
1 tablespoon mayonnaise (or ½ mayonnaise/½ Greek yoghurt)
chopped herbs as available (parsley, fennel or coriander leaves)

Grease a tureen or pan, preferably with olive oil. Place the slices of potato at the bottom, followed by the fish, the carrot and celery. Add the remaining ingredients and simmer, covered, until soft but not mushy, about 20–30 minutes.

To serve, remove from heat. Stir in mayonnaise until the soup looks creamy. Serve immediately sprinkled with fresh chopped parsley, fennel or coriander to taste.

———————————— ◦ ————————————

Michael Spicer, MP
— Member of Parliament for Worcestershire South —

Michael Spicer

SHRIMP AND SOURED CREAM SOUP

Serves 4–6
6 × 150 ml (5 fl. oz) cartons soured cream
1 tablespoon mint sauce
1 × 300–400 g (10–14 oz) can Vichyssoise soup
a drop of Tabasco
salt and freshly ground black pepper
1 small onion, peeled and finely chopped
450 g (1 lb) peeled shrimps

Blend the soured cream, mint sauce, Vichyssoise, Tabasco, salt and pepper. Add finely chopped onion and the whole shrimps. If the soup is too thick, add a little milk.

Chill the soup for a couple of hours in the fridge before serving.

———————————— ◦ ————————————

Rt Hon Gregor Mackenzie
— Ex Member of Parliament for Glasgow, Rutherglen —

Gregor Mackenzie

LENTIL SOUP

Serves 6–8
100 g (¼ lb) lentils, soaked overnight in cold water
225 g (½ lb) carrots, scrubbed and chopped or grated
1.2 litres (2 pints) ham stock (preferably made with ham bones, but stock cubes will do)
salt and freshly ground black pepper

Grind the lentils in a liquidizer (if possible) and put in a pan with the carrots and stock. Cook until soft – about 1 hour – and then pass through a sieve, or liquidize. Season to taste, heat through and serve.

———————————— ○ ————————————

Sir John Stradling Thomas, MP
— Member of Parliament for Monmouth —

John Stradling Thomas.

MONMOUTH LEEK SOUP

Serves 4
8 large leeks, trimmed and washed
40 g (1½ oz) butter
600 ml (1 pint) chicken stock
salt and freshly ground black pepper
20 g (¾ oz) flour
300 ml (½ pint) milk
3 tablespoons single cream

Reserve the pale green top of one of the leeks for a garnish.
Slice the leeks into thin rounds and stir over a gentle heat for 7–8 minutes in half the

butter. Tip in the stock, and season with salt and pepper. Cover and simmer for 10–15 minutes, then liquidize.

Melt the remaining butter in a pan and add the flour off the heat. Stir for a moment, then blend in the milk slowly. Stir until boiling. Add the leek purée and simmer for 3–4 minutes.

Shred the leek top into fine strips about 2.5 cm (1 inch) long and place in a pan of boiling salted water for 5 minutes. Then rinse under cold water to preserve the colour.

Put the cream at the bottom of a warmed tureen and pour in the hot soup. Scatter with warmed leek garnish and serve.

———— ○ ————

Anthony Steen, MP
— MEMBER OF PARLIAMENT FOR SOUTH HAMS —

CARROT AND ORANGE SOUP

SERVES 8
50 g (2 oz) butter
900 g (2 lb) carrots, scraped and thinly sliced
2 onions, peeled and chopped
1 potato, peeled and chopped into 1.25 cm (½ inch) cubes
1.8 litres (3 pints) chicken stock
salt and freshly ground black pepper
2 teaspoons sugar
200 ml (⅓ pint) fresh orange juice
300 ml (½ pint) single cream
snipped chives

Melt the butter in a saucepan and add the carrot, onion and potato. Fry for a few minutes to soften the vegetables. Stir in the stock, seasonings and sugar, then bring to the boil. Cover and simmer gently until all vegetables are soft (10 minutes in a pressure cooker, or 45 minutes in an ordinary saucepan).

Take pan off heat, cool for 10 minutes, then purée the soup in an electric blender. Add the orange juice and cream.

If required hot, reheat to near boiling, sprinkle chives on top, and serve. If required cold, cool and chill for 3 hours. Sprinkle with snipped chives and serve.

———— ○ ————

Ian Mikardo
— Ex Member of Parliament for Bow and Poplar —

TRAWLERMAN'S SOUP

One of my friends can't bear to have put in front of her a plate with a very large quantity of food (however good) on it: she says she's 'overfaced' by it and therefore doesn't feel like starting on it. Reading a recipe book is rather like that: the surfeit dulls the appetite. So this book should be browsed through, never more than one page at a time.

This soup is what my wife puts on the table for me when I get home from the House on a cold winter night after a 10 pm division.

Serves 2
450 g (1 lb) fresh filleted haddock
3 medium potatoes, peeled and cubed
1 small onion, peeled and finely chopped
½ teaspoon sugar
salt and freshly ground black pepper
300 ml (½ pint) milk
butter

Put the fish, potato, onion, sugar, salt and pepper in a pan with 300 ml (½ pint) water, and boil only until the potatoes are almost soft. Add the milk and simmer until the potatoes are quite tender. Serve, adding a dab of butter to each portion.

———————————————— ○ ————————————————

Dr Michael Clark, MP
— Member of Parliament for Rochford —

CURRIED PARSNIP SOUP

A great favourite with family and friends.

Serves 6–8
50 g (2 oz) butter
1 teaspoon curry powder
2 large onions, peeled and chopped
675 g (1½ lb) parsnips, peeled and chopped
600 ml (1 pint) chicken stock
salt and freshly ground white pepper
300 ml (½ pint) milk
150 ml (¼ pint) single cream
GARNISH
diced red apple tossed in lemon juice, or single cream

Melt the butter in a large pan, stir in the curry powder and cook for 2 minutes. Add the onion and parsnip and cook gently for 5 minutes, stirring occasionally. Add the stock, and salt and pepper to taste. Bring to the boil and cook gently for 25–30 minutes, or until the vegetables are tender. Cool slightly.

Sieve, or work in an electric blender, until smooth. Return to the pan and add the milk and cream. Bring to the boil, stirring. Check the seasoning and serve immediately. Garnish with a sprinkling of apple dice per portion or with a swirl of single cream.

———————————— ○ ————————————

Winston S. Churchill, MP
— MEMBER OF PARLIAMENT FOR DAVYHULME —

Winston S Churchill

SQUERRYES GAZPACHO

Serves 4

12 large tomatoes, skinned and seeded	*½ tea cup olive oil*
1 green pepper, seeded and roughly chopped	*¼ tea cup white wine vinegar*
1 red pepper, seeded and roughly chopped	*2 garlic cloves, peeled*
1 large onion, peeled and roughly chopped	*1 × 425 g (15 oz) can consommé*
¼ cucumber, skinned and roughly chopped	*sea salt and freshly ground black pepper to taste*

Blend all the ingredients together in Magimix or blender, and chill. (Alternatively for instant serving, add half a dozen ice cubes to blender.)

Serve with hot, deep-fried bread croûtons.

———————————— ○ ————————————

Jeremy Hanley, MP
— Member of Parliament for Richmond and Barnes —

LAYERED LIVER PÂTÉ WITH CHICKEN

My wife Verna loves cooking for me – but due to our ridiculous hours, pâtés are ideal.

Serves about 8–10
1 onion, peeled and halved
1 bay leaf
300 ml (½ pint) milk
450 g (1 lb) pig's liver, trimmed and roughly chopped
175 g (6 oz) back bacon, rinded and roughly chopped
2 garlic cloves, peeled
¼ teaspoon each of grated nutmeg, ground cloves and crushed allspice berries
1 tablespoon brandy
1 teaspoon green peppercorns
salt and freshly ground black pepper to taste
25 g (1 oz) butter
25 g (1 oz) plain flour
1 egg, beaten
225 g (½ lb) streaky bacon, rinded
1 chicken breast, skinned and boned

Infuse the onion and bay leaf in the warm milk over a gentle heat. Strain after 15 minutes and retain the milk. Mince together (or use a food processor) the liver, back bacon and garlic. Blend in the spices, brandy, peppercorns and salt and pepper to taste.

Make a white sauce using the butter, flour and reserved flavoured milk, then cool. Mix the liver mixture into the white sauce, and add the beaten egg at the same time.

Line a pâté or loaf tin with the rinded streaky bacon rashers, and half-fill with the liver mixture. Put in the chicken breast, then cover with the remaining mixture. Cover with greased paper and place the tin in a roasting pan half-filled with cold water. Bake for 2 hours in a preheated oven at 325°F/160°C/Gas 3. When cooked, pour off excess liquid and leave to cool, weighted down, then refrigerate. May be frozen.

———————— ○ ————————

Archy Kirkwood, MP
— MEMBER OF PARLIAMENT FOR ROXBURGH AND BERWICKSHIRE —

Archy Kirkwood

LIVER PÂTÉ

SERVES 4–6
1 tiny onion, peeled and chopped
15 g (½ oz) butter (or 1 tablespoon oil)
1–2 garlic cloves, peeled and chopped
50 g (2 oz) sausagemeat, chopped
50 g (2 oz) bacon, rinded and chopped
100 g (¼ lb) liver (chicken or lamb's preferably)
breadcrumbs
herbs to taste
salt and freshly ground black pepper to taste
a dash of wine or spirits if liked
a little of anything lying about (eg mushroom stalks)

The quantities above are very approximate.

Fry chopped onion in butter or oil.

Add chopped garlic and stir round.

Add chopped-up sausagemeat and cook well.

Add chopped bacon and cook a bit more.

Add chopped liver and cook only lightly.

Add everything else and cook together for only a minute or two.

Add enough water to liquidize or blend.

Put in bowl and cool.

Serve with Melba toast, wholewheat toast or home-made French loaves (white bread dough rolled into long thin sausages on a baking tin) as a first course, for lunch or for a picnic.

This will freeze happily for a month.

———————— ○ ————————

Rt Hon Michael Cocks
— Ex Member of Parliament for Bristol South —

CHOPPED LIVER

Serves 6
3 medium to large onions, peeled and chopped
corn oil
450 g (1 lb) chicken livers, trimmed
salt and freshly ground black pepper to taste
5 eggs, hard-boiled

Fry onions in a generous amount of oil and then add chicken livers when onions are a light brown in colour. Cook until the livers are cooked through. Season to taste.

Chop the liver, onions and four of the hard-boiled eggs together by hand or, if you are feeling lazy, in the mouli-grater, using the disc with the large holes. If you are feeling *very* lazy, put in the Magimix for 25 seconds, using the white plastic blade. Chop the last egg and sprinkle over the top. If not moist enough, cover with a little more oil.

———————————— ○ ————————————

Mrs Marion Roe, MP
— Member of Parliament for Broxbourne —

CHICKEN LIVER PÂTÉ SUPREME

A delicacy to serve with drinks or with salad at a summer luncheon.

Serves 4
150 g (5 oz) butter
2 onions, peeled and finely chopped
225 g (½ lb) chicken livers, trimmed
2 tablespoons dry sherry
salt

Put 25 g (1 oz) of the butter into a pan and add the onions. Cook slowly until the onion is soft. Add the chicken livers and cook for 10 minutes. Put all in a bowl and mash with a fork (or purée in a blender). Add the sherry to the pan juices and stir and scrape to get up all the good brown bits. Add to the liver then allow to cool.

Cream the remaining butter and then stir in the liver. Season with a little salt and more sherry if needed. Pack into a small bowl and serve with Melba toast.

Gregor Mackenzie, whose recipe for chicken liver pâté was very similar, suggests using only 25–50 g/1–2 oz butter, and port instead of sherry. He says his is very good for use in Beef Wellington, see page 39.

———————————— ○ ————————————

Gerry Neale, MP
— Member of Parliament for Cornwall North —

Gerry Neale

Cornish Smoked Mackerel Pâté

A light, low-fat pâté which is made in a trice in a food processor.

Serves 4–6
2 Cornish smoked mackerel fillets, 350–400 g (12–14 oz) total weight
juice of 1 lemon
½ teaspoon sea salt
freshly ground black pepper
225 g (½ lb) curd (or cream) cheese
125–175 g (4–6 oz) cottage cheese
1–2 pickled cucumbers, roughly chopped, or
2–3 spring onions, chopped (including green part)

Skin the mackerel. (Lay face down, then starting from the tail, the skin should peel off in one piece!) Place the flesh in the food processor or liquidizer. Add lemon juice and seasonings and process briefly. Then add the cheeses plus chopped pickled cucumbers or spring onions, and process again, stirring down. The texture is best not too smooth. More cottage cheese can be added if the mixture is too stiff.

Turn into individual ramekins or a serving dish and refrigerate for at least an hour before serving. This pâté freezes well. Serve decorated with lemon wedges and parsley accompanied by hot granary rolls, toast or crispbread.

———————————— ○ ————————————

Neil Hamilton, MP

— MEMBER OF PARLIAMENT FOR TATTON —

[signature: Neil Hamilton]

TATTON TUNA AND TOMATO PÂTÉ

Very simple – a great stand-by. The pâté freezes superbly and can be used on savoury biscuits as a cocktail snack or as a starter with hot toast.

Serves 6 as a starter
2 × 197 g (7 oz) cans tuna in oil
300 g (10 oz) concentrated tomato purée
juice of 2 large or 3 medium lemons
lots of freshly ground black pepper
double cream or plain yoghurt (optional)

Break up tuna with a fork and place in food processor bowl with tomato purée, lemon juice and pepper. Include the oil with the tuna – or, for dieters, use either tuna in brine (not so delicious) or more lemon juice.

Process according to taste – either until just mixed, giving a coarse pâté, or until completely smooth. The addition of a good dollop of double cream or plain yoghurt is excellent. (The coarse pâté can be made without a food processor just by mixing and mashing with a fork.)

———————— ○ ————————

Michael Marshall, MP
— MEMBER OF PARLIAMENT FOR ARUNDEL —

Michael Marshall.

SMOKED OYSTER MOUSSE

Serves 4
1 × 105 g (3¾ oz) can smoked oysters
1 × 197 g (7 oz) can tuna in oil
1 onion, peeled and finely chopped
250 ml (9 fl. oz) mayonnaise
10 dried sage leaves, crumbled
1 teaspoon freshly ground black pepper
25 g (1 oz) unflavoured gelatine
250 ml (9 fl. oz) hot water
Garnish
cucumber dice

Mix the smoked oysters and tuna with their juices until the tuna is flaked and smooth. Add chopped onion, mayonnaise, sage and pepper.

Dissolve the gelatine in the hot water, then lightly blend with the mixture. Put into a mould and refrigerate until set. Garnish with finely diced cucumber.

Tim Renton, MP
— MEMBER OF PARLIAMENT FOR SUSSEX MID —

Tim Renton

SNAILS

There are three ways of ridding your garden of snails: standing on them, which is messy; feeding them slug pellets, which is ecologically unacceptable; and eating them, which is delicious.

Put several dozen garden snails (the French call them *petit gris* and consider them the best eating variety) under a bucket for a week, with some lettuce leaves, to clean them out.

To cook, drop the snails in boiling water for a minute, then extract them from their shells with a skewer or a snail fork. Wash them in several changes of salted water, until the water runs clear. Simmer for at least 2 hours in fresh water with herbs and seasoning and a glass of wine.

Meanwhile, melt some butter – 25 g (1 oz) per dozen snails – and add fresh (if possible) chopped herbs and some freshly ground pepper. Or you may prefer to add crushed garlic and a little nutmeg.

Put the drained snails back in their shells, or in the holes in china snail dishes, and pour in the butter sauce. Bring to bubbling point under the grill or in a hot oven, and serve at once with French bread. (Cooked snails, with or without sauce, freeze well.)

———————————— ○ ————————————

Hon Mark Lennox-Boyd, MP
— MEMBER OF PARLIAMENT FOR MORECAMBE AND LUNESDALE —

Mark Lennox-Boyd

MORECAMBE BAY SHRIMPS À LA CRÈME

Fresh Morecambe Bay shrimps are one of England's finest fish delicacies. (They should not be confused with the well-known potted variety.) That the fresh shrimps are not more widely known is because they must be eaten no more than a few hours after they are caught. So, come to Morecambe and get them fresh.

Serves 8
900 g (2 lb) fresh shelled Morecambe Bay shrimps
300 ml (½ pint) double cream
juice of 2 lemons
salt and freshly ground black pepper
paprika
2 tablespoons snipped fresh dill

Put the shrimps in a large glass bowl. (A very good supplier is Mr Woodhouse of Morecambe, but they can be purchased in season from most local fishmongers.)

Mix the cream with the lemon juice, salt, pepper, a little paprika and the snipped dill. Mix well with the shrimps and chill before serving.

———————————— ○ ————————————

Mrs Angela Rumbold, CBE, MP
— MEMBER OF PARLIAMENT FOR MITCHAM AND MORDEN —

PLAICE 'CEVICHE'

A very pleasant and be it slightly different starter recipe which the family and many friends have enjoyed for a number of years.

Serves about 4
2 fresh plaice fillets, skinned
1 green pepper, seeded and finely chopped
1 red pepper, seeded and finely chopped
1 avocado pear, peeled, stoned and finely chopped
MARINADE
1 tablespoon Tabasco
1 dessertspoon white wine vinegar
1 small glass white wine
salt and freshly ground black pepper to taste

Cut the plaice into small pieces, and put into a dish with the pepper and avocado dice.

Mix the marinade ingredients together and pour into the dish. Mix, and leave to marinate for 3 hours before serving.

———————————— ○ ————————————

Ms Harriet Harman, MP
— MEMBER OF PARLIAMENT FOR PECKHAM —

Harriet Harman

SAVOURY PANCAKES

Children love mixing the pancake ingredients and spreading on the filling. The trick is to get them to help you make it and then put them to bed before you eat it!

SERVES 4
2 eggs
100 g (¼ lb) wholemeal flour
150 ml (¼ pint) milk
150 ml (¼ pint) light ale
butter

TOPPING
soured cream (or thick plain yoghurt)
flaked smoked mackerel (or any other smoked fish)
snipped chives (or spring onion tops) or red or black lumpfish roe
(fake caviar which can be obtained in most supermarkets)

Mix the eggs, flour, milk and light ale together until smooth, then leave to stand for 1 hour.

Lightly grease a hot frying pan with butter and cook the pancakes on both sides, using ½ ladleful batter at a time.

Spread on to each pancake 2 dessertspoons soured cream or yoghurt and 2 dessertspoons flaked smoked fish. Top with a sprinkling of chives or lumpfish roe.

Mrs Sheila Nicholls

— Personnel Administrator, Refreshment Department, House of Commons —

Sheila L Nicholls

Sheila's Solace

Baked choux pastry does not keep well and should be used within 3–4 hours.

Serves about 6
300 ml (½ pint) water
100 g (¼ lb) butter or margarine
150 g (5 oz) strong plain flour, sifted
salt
4 eggs, size 3
lemon wedges to garnish
Filling
75 g (3 oz) caviar (other roe may be substituted if your budget is stretched!)
Dressing
1 tablespoon each of finely chopped shallots, dill and chives
300 ml (½ pint) soured cream
lemon juice to taste

To make the choux paste, bring the water and fat to the boil in a heavy-based saucepan, then remove from heat. Add the sifted flour and a little salt. Stir vigorously with a wooden spoon until paste is smooth. Cool mixture a little, then beat in the eggs, one at a time. Beat for 3–4 minutes. The paste should be of a dropping consistency.

Place paste into a piping bag with a plain nozzle, and pipe small balls of 2.5 cm (1 inch) in diameter on to dampened baking sheets. Bake in the preheated oven at 400°F/200°C/Gas 6 for 20–30 minutes.

Lift profiteroles off the sheets and prick or slit sides to release the steam. Leave to cool.

Knife open the profiteroles sufficiently to fill with caviar. (Use a small plastic spoon, taking care not to crush the roe.) Arrange profiteroles on a serving dish and garnish with lemon wedges.

Stir shallots, dill and chives into the soured cream, adding lemon juice to taste. Serve dressing separately in a sauce boat.

———————○———————

FISH
AND
SHELLFISH DISHES

Richard Page, MP
— MEMBER OF PARLIAMENT FOR HERTFORDSHIRE SOUTH WEST —

FISH AND AVOCADO ROULADE

Having just lost a stone for the 'weigh-in' for the Spencer's Club lunch, I feel I can indulge myself again with recipes such as this.

SERVES 6
350 g (¾ lb) cod fillet
300 ml (½ pint) fish stock
1 ripe avocado, halved, stoned and peeled
salt and freshly ground black pepper
1 tablespoon snipped fresh dill
5 eggs, separated
FILLING
2 tablespoons thick mayonnaise
1 tablespoon orange lumpfish roe
100 g (¼ lb) smoked salmon, thinly sliced (or chopped trimmings)
snipped dill or chopped parsley

Line a greased Swiss roll tin, approximately 32.5 × 22.5 cm (13 × 9 inches) with greased greaseproof paper.

Poach the cod fillet in fish stock until just tender, then drain thoroughly and remove any bones. Blend the cooked fish briefly in the food processor with the avocado flesh. Season to taste with salt and pepper and beat in the snipped dill and the egg yolks.

Whisk the egg whites until stiff but not dry, and fold carefully into the fish mixture. Pour into the prepared tin, easing it to the edges so that it fills the tin evenly.

Bake in a preheated oven at 350°F/180°C/Gas 4 for 18–20 minutes until firm but spongy to the touch. Turn out on to a fresh sheet of greaseproof paper and lay a damp teatowel over the bottom lining paper. Leave to cool for an hour. Remove the teatowel and carefully peel the lining paper away from the roulade.

Mix the mayonnaise with the lumpfish roe and some salt and pepper, to taste. Spread over the roulade evenly and lay the smoked salmon slices or pieces on top. Roll up as for a Swiss roll and sprinkle with dill or parsley. Serve cold, in slices.

———————— ○ ————————

Sir Geoffrey Johnson Smith, DL, MP
— MEMBER OF PARLIAMENT FOR WEALDEN —

Geoffrey Johnson Smith

'POACHED' SALMON

There is no doubt that the recipe is considerably enhanced if you purchase a line, find a suitable beat and catch the fish yourself. But no cook or chef can possibly improve the taste of a fish so much as the imagination of an angler. I am also certain that the ones that get away would taste even nicer!

SERVES 6
1 salmon
1 tablespoon double cream
2 lemons, sliced thinly
chopped parsley
salt and freshly ground black pepper

Clean the salmon thoroughly, and place on a piece of buttered foil large enough to enclose it completely. Put the cream inside the cavity and cover this with half the lemon slices and a generous sprinkling of chopped parsley. Season to taste.

Arrange the remaining lemon slices along the top side of the salmon. Bring the foil around the fish and seal loosely. Cook in the preheated oven between 375–400°F/190°–200°C/Gas 5–6 for 40–55 minutes. Take from oven, remove foil and lemon, and peel.

Serve hot with hollandaise sauce. If serving cold, garnish when cold with cucumber and wedges of lemon. Serve with mayonnaise or green sauce.

———————————— ○ ————————————

Rt Hon Norman St John-Stevas
— EX MEMBER OF PARLIAMENT FOR CHELMSFORD —

Norman St J St-Stevas

SOLE IN CHAMPAGNE SAUCE

This recipe is ideal for using up leftover champagne.

Serves 4
4 large fillets of sole (or flounder), skinned
salt and freshly ground black pepper
butter
125 ml (4 fl. oz) champagne
50 g (2 oz) boiled or canned shrimps, finely chopped

Wash the skinned fillets thoroughly, then blot dry. Season to taste with salt and pepper. Lay them in a fireproof serving/baking dish and dot liberally with butter.

Sauté on top of the stove for 8–10 minutes, then pour on the champagne, and sprinkle with the chopped shrimps. Transfer to a preheated oven (350°F/180°C/Gas 4) and bake for 10 minutes, or until the fillets are tender.

———————————— ○ ————————————

Barry Henderson
— Ex Member of Parliament for Fife North East —

East Neuk Fish

Serves 4–6
450–900 g (1–2 lb) white fish fillets
milk
25 g (1 oz) margarine
1 onion, peeled and finely chopped
25 g (1 oz) plain flour
about 25–50 g (1–2 oz) Cheddar cheese
100 g (¼ lb) shelled prawns
100 g (¼ lb) cooked shelled mussels

Place the fish in a pan and just cover with milk. Bring gently to simmering point and simmer for about 5 minutes. Break into large pieces, removing any skin and bones, and remove from the pan with a slotted spoon to a serving dish. Keep warm.

Heat the margarine in a pan, and fry the onion gently until soft. Add the flour, mix in well and then gradually add the fish juices, mixing well until smooth. Add enough extra milk to make a sauce that will cover the fish. Grate in just enough cheese to flavour the sauce. Add the prawns and mussels and, when hot, pour over the fish.

———————————— ○ ————————————

Rt Hon Edward Heath, MBE, MP

— MEMBER OF PARLIAMENT FOR OLD BEXLEY AND SIDCUP —

Edward Heath

TRUITE À L'EDWARD

Cette truite est un 'treat'.

SERVES 4
4 fresh trout
50 g (2 oz) butter
2 tablespoons olive oil
25 g (1 oz) shallots, peeled and finely chopped
1 egg
200 g (7 oz) breadcrumbs from French bread
200 g (7 oz) button mushrooms, finely chopped
lots of chopped parsley
salt and freshly ground black pepper
150 ml (¼ pint) white wine
150 ml (¼ pint) single cream

Clean the trout thoroughly. Heat butter and oil in a frying pan, add shallots, and gently sauté to brown them. Break the egg into the breadcrumbs and mix with the chopped mushrooms, shallots and most of the parsley. Add salt and pepper to taste.

Stuff the trout with this mixture. Carefully place the trout, stuffed side upright, in the pan. Add wine and more parsley. Cover and cook slowly for 15–20 minutes.

When cooked, place the trout on a plate and keep warm. Add the cream to the cooking juices and stir, but do not allow to boil. Pour sauce over trout and serve hot.

———————————— ○ ————————————

Ann Lunn, Personal Assistant to the General Manager, Refreshment Department, House of Commons, poaches trout in a moderate oven for 20–25 minutes, along with boiled and halved leeks. The fish and leeks are covered with a sauce made from a roux of butter and flour, the fish juices, white wine and double cream or sheep's milk yoghurt, then sprinkled with breadcrumbs and browned under the grill.

Dennis Walters, MBE, MP
— Member of Parliament for Westbury —

Walters Family Mussels

This is a delicious and cheap dish which is excellent for supper served with crusty or French bread. It is very simple, but cleaning the mussels is fairly time-consuming which can make one reluctant to do it for more than four people.

Serves 2
2.25 litres (2 quarts/4 pints) mussels (which makes allowances for discards)
50 g (2 oz) butter
1 medium onion, peeled and finely chopped
1 garlic clove, peeled and chopped (optional)
freshly ground black pepper
1 glass white wine
about 60–85 ml (2–3 fl. oz) single cream
finely chopped fresh parsley

Scrape, scrub and thoroughly clean the mussels in fresh water. If buying them, they often come in bags already semi-cleaned. Throw away any which float or are open or damaged. It is important to change the water several times to make sure you have got rid of all the grit.

Melt the butter and fry the onion gently in a large saucepan or casserole with a well fitting lid; add garlic as and if you like – I never do. When the onion is transparent, grind in some pepper and pour in the white wine; let it bubble a minute. Now add the mussels and slam on the lid, turning up the heat as high as it will go. Shake the pan once or twice, and after about 4 minutes look. It is ready if all the shells are wide open. (Discard any that are still closed after a few seconds more cooking.)

Pour in the cream and shake the pan again, letting the cream cook for about a minute. Ladle the mussels into individual bowls. Strain the liquid over them carefully, because, in spite of your cleaning, it may still be gritty.

Sprinkle the chopped parsley over the shells and serve, providing another dish for empty shells. It should need no salt if the mussels are fresh and have recently been living in the sea. If they were bought, they do sometimes need a little salt, but I think it is safer to leave it to individual taste and let each add their own if necessary.

———————————— ○ ————————————

Nicholas Baker, MP
— MEMBER OF PARLIAMENT FOR DORSET NORTH —

Nicholas Baker

SALMON LOAF

A superb all-singing all-dancing stand-by which my wife Carol serves hot or cold. Ideal for supporters requiring a light meal and political discussion.

SERVES 4–6

75 g (3 oz) breadcrumbs
150 ml (¼ pint) milk
1 × 210 g (7½ oz) can salmon

2 eggs, beaten
salt and freshly ground black pepper
2 teaspoons lemon juice

Soak the breadcrumbs in the milk. Tip the salmon into a basin and mash together with the liquid from the can. Add it to the milk and breadcrumbs, then add the beaten eggs, salt, pepper and lemon juice.

Mix well – if you have a blender, all the ingredients can be combined in a matter of seconds – then check the seasoning. Pour into a greased 450 g (1 lb) loaf tin or foil container, and bake for 45 minutes at 350°F/180°C/Gas 4 until set. Cool.

If served warm, it is nice cut into slices with cooked and sliced cucumber and new potatoes or stir-fried vegetables. If served cold, it is nice with a salad and yoghurt-type dressing.

To freeze, cover with foil, seal and label. Use within 1 month. Thaw overnight in the fridge, turn out and cut into slices.

———————————— ○ ————————————

Roland Boyes, MP
— MEMBER OF PARLIAMENT FOR HOUGHTON AND WASHINGTON —

Roland Boyes

SUPPER SALMON

I don't know the source of the recipe. It's one of the 'good'uns' that gets passed on – and probably changes a bit along the way.

Serves 4
1 × 450 g (1 lb) can salmon
25 g (1 oz) butter
1 small onion, peeled and finely chopped
1 medium green pepper, seeded and finely chopped
1 can condensed cream of mushroom soup
3 tablespoons milk
50–75 g (2–3 oz) coarse breadcrumbs
1 tablespoon grated Parmesan cheese

Drain the salmon and remove skin and bones. Break flesh into good-sized chunks and place in a small greased casserole.

Heat the butter in a small frying pan and lightly sauté the onion and the pepper. Add soup and milk, blend well and heat to almost boiling.

Pour mixture over the salmon, cover with breadcrumbs and sprinkle with cheese. Bake for 20 minutes in a hot oven at 400°F/200°C/Gas 6.

It's good enough to eat on its own, better with new potatoes and broccoli, and perhaps better again with a vegetable rice.

—————————— ○ ——————————

Hon Greville Janner, QC, MP
— MEMBER OF PARLIAMENT FOR LEICESTER WEST —

[signature]

GEFILTE FISH

Chopped fish balls (Gefilte fish) are an essential item of the Jewish diet. In Central Europe and in Israel, they are traditionally made with carp, which (for both culinary and linguistic reasons) MPs may prefer to substitute for haddock (see below). Whether boiled (as below) or fried, they should be soft. If yours emerge tough or chewy, please try again.

SERVES ABOUT 4–6
fish trimmings (see below)
2 large carrots, peeled
1 large onion, peeled and chopped
FISH BALLS
900 g (2 lb) raw fish, minced (filleted haddock or cod)
225 g (½ lb) minced onion
2 tablespoons oil
salt and freshly ground black pepper
3 large eggs
6 tablespoons medium matzo meal

Ask fishmonger for bones and skin of a cleaned hake, or a haddock head. Put in cold water with peeled carrots and chopped onion. Boil for 10–15 minutes while you are making the fish balls.

Mix all the fish ball ingredients together and with wet hands mould into medium apple-sized shapes. Put into stock and simmer for 1¼ hours.

Remove the balls with a slotted spoon, and put into a 2.5 cm (1 inch) deep dish. Strain the stock and pour over balls. Cut the carrots in slices and put a piece on each ball.

———————————— ○ ————————————

Gerald Malone, ex MP for Aberdeen South, offers a quick dish for after a busy day. Mix drained crab meat, prawns and a little mustard into thick, whipped double cream. Roll the mixture in bacon rashers and grill for 7 minutes.

Anthony Nelson, MP
— MEMBER OF PARLIAMENT FOR CHICHESTER —

SELSEY FISH PIE

Following my Adjournment Debate plea to the Minister for Fisheries, the ban on cod fishing off Selsey was lifted. Connoisseurs of seafood rejoiced that this delectable fish pie could once more be savoured!

SERVES 6
675 g (1½ lb) fillet of Selsey cod, skinned (inferior alternatives may be used)
350 g (¾ lb) smoked haddock, skinned
milk to cover
100 g (¼ lb) shelled prawns
100 g (¼ lb) button mushrooms, washed and quartered
4 hard-boiled eggs, quartered
butter
plain flour
salt and freshly ground black pepper
approx. 250–350 g (½–¾ lb) cooked, creamy, mashed potato

Put Selsey cod and haddock in a pan with just enough milk to cover. Put the lid on, bring slowly to the boil, then remove from the heat and leave covered for a few minutes. Drain the fish, reserving the flavoured milk. Remove any bones from the fish, flake the flesh, and place in a warm serving dish with prawns, mushrooms and quartered hard-boiled eggs.

Make a white sauce with butter and flour, using the milk in which the fish was cooked. Season well. Add to the ingredients in the serving dish and mix gently.

Top the whole with creamy mashed potato. Dot with knobs of butter and brown under the grill.

———————— o ————————

Instead of a potato topping as here, or a scone dough one as on page 37, Bob McTaggart, Member of Parliament for Glasgow Central, suggests a cheesy choux pastry topping for a simple fish stew. Add grated Parmesan and Gruyère to a basic choux paste, place in dessertspoon-sized heaps around the dish, and bake in a preheated hot oven until brown. David Porter, MP for Waveney, suggests adding soured cream, butter and freshly grated nutmeg to the potato topping for a fish pie – in his case, made with fish landed in Lowestoft, 'the foremost fish market in Britain'!

Rt Hon Merlyn Rees, PC, MP
— MEMBER OF PARLIAMENT FOR LEEDS SOUTH AND MORLEY —

Merly Rees

FISH TIMBALE

SERVES 4
450 g (1 lb) cooked potato
butter
2 eggs
salt and freshly ground black pepper
225 g (½ lb) any white filleted fish, skinned
milk
plain flour
1 teaspoon anchovy essence
GARNISH
2 tomatoes, washed
1 hard-boiled egg, cut into eighths

Push the potato through a sieve whilst hot, then add 40 g (1½ oz) of the butter, one of the eggs, beaten, and salt and pepper to taste. Heat all together, beating well. Turn on to a floured board and roll into a long sausage about 5 cm (2 inches) thick. Place on a greased baking tray, join the two ends and form into a round or oval shape, patting it until it is about 7.5–10 cm (3–4 inches) high. Brush with the remaining egg, beaten, and bake near the top of an oven set at 400°F/200°C/Gas 6 for 20 minutes. Leave until a good golden brown.

At the same time, quarter the garnish tomatoes, place them in a greased tin and heat through in the oven for 20 minutes.

Meanwhile, cook the fish in milk as in the previous recipe. Flake and remove any bones, reserving the flavoured milk as before.

Make a white sauce with butter, flour and reserved milk. Add the flaked fish, anchovy essence and salt and pepper to taste.

When the potato border is brown, lift it carefully on to a hot dish. Fill it with the fish filling, and garnish with hard-boiled egg and tomato quarters. Serve immediately.

———————————— ○ ————————————

John Townend, MP for Bridlington, poaches smoked and fresh haddock in milk with seasonings and lemon rind. A white sauce made with the flavoured milk is poured over the flaked fish. The dish is covered with sliced, butter-cooked mushrooms, sliced tomatoes and grated cheese, and baked in a low oven for 30 minutes. Grill to brown.

Peter Rost, MP
— Member of Parliament for Erewash —

GREEN SEA PIE

This dish keeps hot without spoiling and is delicious served with green beans or broccoli and new potatoes. Any leftovers can be heated up or eaten cold!

Serves 4–6
450–675 g (1–1½ lb) mixed fish, preferably including haddock, cod and whiting
225 g (½ lb) shelled prawns
court-bouillon (fish stock)
1 medium onion, peeled and finely chopped
1 can mussels in brine (or fresh cooked), drained
100 g (¼ lb) tiny button mushrooms (or a small can)
butter
plain flour
150 ml (¼ pint) white wine
Scone pastry
450–675 g (1–1½ lb) self-raising flour (according to size of dish to be covered)
1 teaspoon each of dried parsley, thyme and tarragon (or 1 dessertspoon chopped of each if fresh)
1–1½ teaspoons salt
175–250 g (6–9 oz) butter
about 300–450 ml (½–¾ pint) milk
a little lemon juice

Simmer the fish and prawns in court-bouillon to cover until just cooked. Remove the fish and prawns with a slotted spoon and arrange in a fairly large quiche or pie dish. Reserve the fish liquid. Add the onion, drained mussels and whole mushrooms to the fish.

Make a sauce with butter, flour and the fish liquid, adding the white wine at last. Cook to thicken and pour over the fish.

To make the pastry, mix flour, herbs and salt and rub in butter, then add just enough of the milk and lemon juice to make a soft dough. Knead a little until smooth then roll out on a floured board to fit the dish, about 1.25 cm (½ inch) thick. Put it on the dish and, using a sharp knife, mark the pastry into portions, brush with a little milk, and cook in a fairly hot oven – about 425°F/220°C/Gas 7 – until golden, with green specks from the herbs!

───────────── ○ ─────────────

Meat Dishes

Rt Hon Norman Tebbit, MP
— MEMBER OF PARLIAMENT FOR CHINGFORD —

BEEF WELLINGTON

I have always enjoyed Beef Wellington not merely for its culinary delight, but because of the memory of such a great man. After all, to have named after one a piece of footwear, a great city, and a great dish, is almost enough without that of the battles won, or what endears me most of all to the man – his classic injunction to a would-be blackmailer, 'Publish and be damned!'

SERVES 4
900 g (2 lb) fillet of beef, well trimmed
freshly ground black pepper
25 g (1 oz) butter
100 g (¼ lb) button mushrooms, sliced
1 dessertspoon chopped mixed herbs and parsley
salt
225 g (½ lb) puff pastry
225 g (½ lb) smooth pâté of choice
beaten egg, to glaze
watercress, to garnish

Tie up the fillet so that it will have a neat shape. Sprinkle with pepper, brown it quickly all over in an ovenproof pan in the hot butter, then roast in the preheated hot oven (425°F/220°C/Gas 7) for 10 minutes. Take out and allow to get cold.

Sauté the sliced mushrooms in the butter remaining in the pan for a few minutes, then remove from the heat. Add the mixed herbs and salt to taste, then leave to cool.

Roll the puff pastry out to a thin rectangle and divide in two, one piece two-thirds larger than the other (large enough to almost cover the beef). Put the mushroom mixture on to this large piece, spreading it to the size of the beef.

Cut the fillet in half lengthways and spread the pâté on the cut side of one half. Top with the other half then put the whole thing on to the mushroom mixture. Press the pastry around the fillet and then lay the other piece of pastry over the top. Press to seal, using a little egg glaze if necessary, then brush all over with egg. Decorate with 'fleurons' or leaves made from excess pastry, and egg glaze again.

Bake in the hot oven as above for 30–40 minutes or until well browned. Serve hot or cold, garnished with watercress.

———————— ○ ————————

I. Gabay
— EXECUTIVE CHEF, REFRESHMENT DEPARTMENT, HOUSE OF COMMONS —

FILLET STEAK WESTMINSTER

Per person
1 fillet steak, about 175–200 g (6–7 oz)
25 g (1 oz) liver pâté or goose liver pâté
25 g (1 oz) Parma or Bayonne ham, cut very thin
15 g (½ oz) butter
freshly ground black pepper
1 shallot, peeled and finely chopped
25 g (1 oz) button mushrooms, thinly sliced
2 medium tomatoes, skinned and chopped
25 ml (1 fl. oz) dry sherry or Madeira
75 ml (2½ fl. oz) double cream
1 sprig each of fresh tarragon and parsley, finely chopped
salt

Make an incision in the side of the fillet steak, insert the pâté, then wrap the ham around the steak.

Heat the butter in a sauté pan until fairly hot. Season steak with black pepper and cook for 4 minutes on each side. Place steak on a serving dish and keep hot.

Add the shallot and mushroom to the butter left in the pan and cook slowly for 5 minutes, then add the tomatoes, alcohol and cream. Bring to the boil, then add chopped herbs and correct seasoning, adding some salt if necessary. Pour sauce over steak and serve immediately.

———————————————○———————————————

Rt Hon Michael R. D. Heseltine, MP
— MEMBER OF PARLIAMENT FOR HENLEY —

STEAK AND KIDNEY PIE

SERVES 6
675 g (1½ lb) stewing steak, trimmed and cubed
225 g (½ lb) kidney, skinned, cored and cubed
oil or dripping
1 medium onion, peeled and sliced
2 heaped tablespoons plain flour
2 tablespoons tomato purée
600–900 ml (1–1½ pints) stock
150 ml (¼ pint) red wine
100 g (¼ lb) mushrooms, sliced
chopped fresh parsley
a large pinch of dried basil (or fresh)
salt and freshly ground black pepper
350 g (¾ lb) puff pastry
1 egg, beaten

Put the steak and kidney into a fireproof dish and fry in the oil or dripping briefly. Add the onion and fry until softened. Sprinkle the flour over the meat and onion, then put into a hot oven (375–400°F/190–200°C/Gas 5–6) with the top off for 5 minutes to allow the flour to soak up the fat. Remove from the oven and mix in the tomato purée. Add the stock, wine, mushrooms, chopped parsley and basil. Bring to the boil, cover and simmer for 1 hour. Add salt and pepper to taste and put into a pie dish.

Roll out the pastry and cut a strip to put round the edge of the dish. Brush with water and put the bulk of the pastry on top. Cut round the sides carefully with a knife, 'knock up' with the back of a knife, and decorate the top with leaves made from the pastry trimmings. Brush with beaten egg to glaze and put into a hot oven at the same temperature as above. Bake for 30–35 minutes until the pastry is puffed and brown.

Derek Barnett
— The Times —

Derek Barnett

STEAK AND KIDNEY HOTPOT

SERVES 6–8
675 g (1½ lb) skirt or shin of beef, trimmed and cut into 1.25 cm (½ inch) dice
1 tablespoon dripping
225 g (½ lb) ox kidney, skinned, cored and diced
1 rounded tablespoon plain flour
1 medium onion, peeled and finely chopped
100 g (¼ lb) mushrooms, sliced
salt and freshly ground black pepper
450 ml (¾ pint) stock
450–675 g (1–1½ lb) potatoes, peeled and sliced
25–50 g (1–2 oz) butter (or dripping)

Brown beef quickly in dripping and draw aside. Roll kidney in flour. Pack meat, kidney, onion and mushroom into a thick casserole with plenty of seasoning.

Pour on stock, cover with a tight-fitting lid, and cook slowly in the preheated oven at 325°F/160°C/Gas 3 for 2–3 hours, or until meat is tender. After the first hour cover the meat with a thick layer of potatoes, and dot with butter (or dripping). Cover and continue cooking. Remove lid a good 30 minutes before meat is cooked to allow potatoes to become crusty.

———————— ○ ————————

Cyril Smith, MBE, MP
— MEMBER OF PARLIAMENT FOR ROCHDALE —

BEEF HOT POT

This dish is better known as 'Currie-ho!' and does wonders for the figure – just look at me!

Serves 4–6
450 g (1 lb) beef chuck steak, cut into 2.5 cm (1 inch) pieces
3 teaspoons salt
a little oil or dripping
150 ml (¼ pint) water
6 medium potatoes and carrots, peeled and sliced
4 medium onions, peeled and sliced
½ teaspoon Tabasco
1 × 450 g (1 lb) can tomatoes

Sprinkle beef with a little of the salt, then brown thoroughly in a frying pan in the fat. Remove beef. Add the water to fat in pan and cook, stirring continuously, to blend bits of meat left in pan. Remove from heat.

Layer beef, potatoes, carrots and onions in a casserole, sprinkling each layer with salt and a little Tabasco, and adding some tomato to each layer. Finish with a layer of potatoes, and pour water and fat over. Cook at 350°F/180°C/Gas 4 for at least 2 hours.

———————————— ○ ————————————

Robin Squire, MP
— Member of Parliament for Hornchurch —

CORNED BEEF HASH

Serves 4–6
75 g (3 oz) butter
1 onion, peeled and finely chopped
350 g (¾ lb) canned corned beef, diced
1 large cooked beetroot, peeled and diced

350 g (¾ lb) boiled potatoes, peeled and diced
2–4 tablespoons tomato ketchup
2 teaspons Worcestershire sauce
salt and freshly ground black pepper
2–4 tablespoons double cream

Melt 50 g (2 oz) of the butter in a large pan over moderate heat. Add chopped onion and cook for 3–5 minutes until softened, stirring frequently. Combine beef, beetroot and potatoes in a mixing bowl. Add softened onion, tomato ketchup and Worcestershire sauce, and mix well. Season generously with salt and pepper. Turn into the pan and cook over a moderate heat, stirring, for about 5 minutes or until golden brown.

Using a wooden spoon or spatula, gently pat the hash into a cake in the pan. Dot with the remaining butter and sprinkle with cream. Place under a very hot grill until the top is crisp and golden. Cut into wedges and serve immediately.

———————————— ○ ————————————

Tom Torney
— Ex Member of Parliament for Bradford South —

Tom Torney (signature)

STEAK TOM

If you prefer, you can throw away the steak and veg and drink the gravy – it is lovely!

Serves 2
450 g (1 lb) sirloin steak in one piece
25 g (1 oz) butter
salt and freshly ground black pepper
100 g (¼ lb) mushrooms, peeled and finely chopped
3 tomatoes, skinned and finely chopped
1 small onion, peeled and finely chopped
a considerable quantity of red wine (preferably Modri Burgundunac, Yugoslavia)

Beat the steak and cut it into two portions.

Melt half the butter in a frying pan over a low heat. Sprinkle with salt and pepper to taste, then add the mushrooms, tomatoes and onion along with a liberal quantity of the wine. Cook until a mushy substance.

Salt and pepper the steaks and melt remaining butter in another pan. Cook steak in pan over a low heat for a few minutes then turn it over and pour over liberal quantities of the wine. Cook to taste, then pour in the cooked mushroom, tomato and onion mixture.

Pour more wine over the now full frying pan and allow the wine to heat up.

———————————— ○ ————————————

Rt Hon Sir James Callaghan
— Ex Member of Parliament for Cardiff South and Penarth —

James Callaghan (signature)

MOUSSAKA

My wife uses this recipe from time to time, and it certainly makes a very nice dish.

Serves 10–12

4 medium aubergines	a handful of sultanas
salt	2–3 eggs, beaten
50 g (2 oz) butter	25 g (1 oz) breadcrumbs
900 g (2 lb) ground beef	cooking oil
3 onions, peeled and chopped	50 g (2 oz) Cheddar cheese, grated
2 tablespoons tomato purée	*Sauce*
1 tablespoon freshly chopped parsley	75 g (3 oz) butter
125 ml (4 fl. oz) red wine	6 tablespoons plain flour
freshly ground black pepper	750 ml (1¼ pints) hot milk
50 ml (2 fl. oz) water	a dash of grated nutmeg
a dash of ground cinnamon	4 egg yolks, lightly beaten

Remove 1.25 cm (½ inch) wide strips of peel lengthwise from aubergines, leaving 1.25 cm (½ inch) between the strips. Cut into thick slices, sprinkle with salt, and let stand between two heavy plates while browning the meat and making the sauce.

In a frying pan melt the 50 g (2 oz) butter and in it sauté the meat and onion until meat is browned. Add tomato purée, parsley, wine, some salt, the pepper and water. Simmer until liquid is absorbed. Cool. Stir in cinnamon, sultanas, eggs, and half the crumbs.

To make the sauce, melt the 75 g (3 oz) butter in a saucepan over a low heat. Add flour, and stir until well blended. Remove from the heat. Gradually stir in the hot milk. Return to heat and cook, stirring, until the sauce is thick and smooth. Add some salt and pepper to taste and the nutmeg. Combine the egg yolks with a little of the hot sauce, then stir egg mixture into the sauce and cook over a very low heat for 2 minutes, stirring constantly.

Rinse the aubergine slices and pat dry. Brown them on both sides in hot oil. Grease an ovenproof casserole and sprinkle the bottom with the remaining breadcrumbs. Cover with a layer of aubergine slices, then a layer of meat and continue layering until all aubergine and meat is used, finishing with a layer of aubergine. Cover with sauce, sprinkle with grated cheese and bake in the oven at 350°F/180°C/Gas 4 for 1 hour. Serve hot.

Rupert Allason, MP
— Member of Parliament for Torbay —

Rupert Allason

BEEF AND CHUTNEY

Beef and Chutney is almost impossible to ruin. It actually seems to improve the longer it cooks. A useful late-night supper dish – could be renamed 'Division Stew'!

SERVES ANY NUMBER

good quality stewing steak (no fat)
seasoned flour
dripping
red wine

port
mango chutney
carrots, peeled and chopped
small onions, peeled and chopped

Coat the steak pieces in seasoned flour and seal in a frying pan containing the dripping. Transfer to a casserole dish and cover with red wine, a good dollop of port and a couple of tablespoons of chutney. Cook in a slow oven for several hours.

It actually improves if cooked the day before you want it and simply reheated for another hour or so, adding the chopped carrots and onions.

———————————— ○ ————————————

Jerry Wiggin, TD, MP
— Member of Parliament for Weston-super-Mare —

LAMB CHOPS

This recipe requires no thought or skill and is therefore eminently suitable for political cooks.

lamb chops
Lea and Perrins Worcestershire sauce
redcurrant jelly

For each lamb chop, 1 dessertspoon of Worcestershire sauce and 1 dessertspoon of redcurrant jelly. Place on chops in covered casserole dish in oven at 400–425°F/200–220°C/Gas 6–7 for 1 hour. Stir once or twice. Can be served direct from casserole. Gravy is ready made.

———————————○———————————

Sir Eldon Griffiths, MP
— MEMBER OF PARLIAMENT FOR BURY ST EDMUNDS —

CASSEROLED LAMB CHOPS WITH MUSHROOMS

This can be cooked the day before and reheated.

SERVES 2/SERVES 6
4/12 best end of neck lamb chops, trimmed
40 g (1½ oz)/65 g (2½ oz) butter
100 g (¼ lb)/350 g (¾ lb) mushrooms, washed
2/4 tablespoons redcurrant jelly
1/2 tablespoons Worcestershire sauce
1/3 tablespoons lemon juice
a pinch/¼ teaspoon grated nutmeg
salt and freshly ground black pepper
1/2 dessertspoons plain flour
150 ml (¼ pint)/300 ml (½ pint) meat stock

Brown the chops quickly in the butter in a frying pan. Transfer them to a casserole and put the mushrooms on top.

In a saucepan, slowly melt the redcurrant jelly with the Worcestershire sauce and lemon juice. Add the nutmeg and seasonings.

Add the flour to the fat in the frying pan and blend in the stock and mixture from the saucepan. Bring to the boil and cook for 2 minutes. Adjust seasoning and pour over the cutlets.

Cook in a low oven at 300°F/150°C/Gas 2 for 1¼ hours. When cooked, cool and chill in the refrigerator overnight.

The next day, reheat in a moderate oven at 350°F/180°C/Gas 4 for about 25 minutes.

———————————○———————————

Rt Hon Cecil Parkinson, MP
— MEMBER OF PARLIAMENT FOR HERTSMERE —

LANCASHIRE HOT POT

SERVES 4–6
900 g (2 lb) lamb best end of neck, trimmed and cut into small pieces
25 g (1 oz) dripping
2 large onions, peeled and chopped
4 large potatoes, peeled and sliced
salt and freshly ground black pepper
600 ml (1 pint) beef stock

Brown meat in dripping in a frying pan.

Place a layer of meat in the bottom of a heavy casserole, then a layer of onions, followed by a layer of potatoes. Continue thus until all the ingredients are used up, finishing with a layer of potatoes completely covering top. Season with salt and pepper between layers. Add the beef stock down the side of the casserole: it should come right up to the top potato layer, but if not, top up with water.

Simmer, covered, for 2 hours on top of the stove, or for 2½ hours in the oven at 350°F/180°C/Gas 4.

Before serving, place under a hot grill to brown and crisp the top layer of potatoes.

———————————————— ○ ————————————————

Rt Hon Tom King, MP
— MEMBER OF PARLIAMENT FOR BRIDGWATER —

WEST COUNTRY SUMMER PORK

(Note: Peter Rost, MP for Erewash, also uses cider in a pork stew – which 'is made in our house with our own home-made "70% proof" scrumpy!')

Serves 6
1.1 kg (2½ lb) pork, boned and cubed
plain flour
salt and freshly ground black pepper
2 tablespoons oil
225 g (½ lb) onions, peeled and finely chopped
1 garlic clove, peeled and chopped (optional)
225 g (½ lb) carrots, scrubbed and sliced
1 stock cube (pork, chicken or lamb flavour), crumbled
1 bouquet garni
225 g (½ lb) green beans, topped and tailed
1 tablespoon lemon juice
450 g (1 lb) small new potatoes, scrubbed
at least 300 ml (½ pint) Taunton or scrumpy cider

Dust pork with flour seasoned with salt and pepper. Fry pork in oil to seal, then remove with a slotted spoon and place in a large casserole. Lightly fry onions, garlic (if used) and carrots in oil left in pan. Sprinkle with 1 tablespoon of seasoned flour to take up juices. Add to the pork in the casserole, then add everything except the cider. Mix well, then gently cover with cider.

Cover the casserole and cook in the preheated oven at 325°F/160°C/Gas 3 for 2–2½ hours. Serve with broccoli.

———————— ○ ————————

Bryan Gould, MP
— MEMBER OF PARLIAMENT FOR DAGENHAM —

PORK WITH JUNIPER BERRIES AND DATES

SERVES 4
675 g (1½ lb) pork fillet, trimmed and cubed
1 large onion, peeled and finely chopped
1 teaspoon oil
1 teaspoon ground allspice
6 juniper berries, ground in a mortar
salt and freshly ground black pepper
50 g (2 oz) mushrooms, sliced
25 g (1 oz) chopped dates
1 glass red wine
1 teaspoon cornflour mixed in 85 ml (3 fl. oz) cream

Sauté the pork and onion in the oil in a large pan. Mix the allspice and juniper berries together, add to the pan, and season with salt and pepper to taste. Stir and add mushrooms, dates and red wine, and cook over a high heat until the liquid is syrupy.

Reduce the heat, cover and cook gently for about 30 minutes. Add cornflour and cream mixture, and simmer for a few minutes to heat through and thicken slightly. Test for seasoning and add any further liquid to produce a sauce of the desired consistency.

—————————— ○ ——————————

Hon Mrs Gwyneth Dunwoody, MP
— MEMBER OF PARLIAMENT FOR CREWE AND NANTWICH —

WELSH SUPPER PIE

When I had small children they loved this good solid old farmhouse food – and they still do – but now we have to use my grandchildren as the excuse!

Serves 4–6
450 g (1 lb) pork sausagemeat
2 bacon rashers, rinded and diced
1 cooking apple, peeled, cored and diced
450 g (1 lb) cooked mashed potato
15 g (½ oz) butter
1 tablespoon cream (optional)
225–450 g (½–1 lb) good strong Red Leicester cheese, grated

Place a layer of sausagemeat in a casserole. Lightly fry the bacon in a frying pan in its own fat. Mix with the apple dice and sprinkle on top of sausagemeat. Mash the potato further with the butter and, if required, a tablespoon of cream, and smooth on top of the ingredients in the casserole. Sprinkle with cheese (as much as you like), and bake in a medium oven at about 350°F/180°C/Gas 4 for 45 minutes.

———————————— ○ ————————————

Mark Wolfson, MP
— MEMBER OF PARLIAMENT FOR SEVENOAKS —

VERONICA VEAL

Serves 2/Serves 6
2/6 thin fillets of veal, about 100 g (¼ lb) each
plain flour
salt and freshly ground black pepper
50 g (2 oz)/100 g (¼ lb) butter
½/1½ wine glass(es) white wine
12/36 white grapes, skinned and pipped
3 tablespoons/300 ml (½ pint) single cream
2/5 tablespoons mild English cheese, grated

Roll the veal fillets in the flour seasoned with salt and pepper.

Heat butter in frying pan and cook veal fillets for 3 minutes on either side. Remove pan from the heat and stir in wine, grapes, cream and salt and pepper to taste.

Transfer to a heatproof dish and sprinkle with grated cheese. Cook in a very low oven at about 275°F/140°C/Gas 1 for 20 minutes, and then brown top under grill immediately before serving. (This last step is not essential.)

———————————— ○ ————————————

Stephen Ross
— Ex Member of Parliament for Isle of Wight —

SAUSAGE AND APPLE PIE

SERVES 2–4
shortcrust pastry made with approx. 225 g (½ lb) wholemeal flour
225 g (½ lb) good quality pork sausagemeat
1 teaspoon dried sage
2 medium onions, peeled
1 large Bramley apple, peeled, cored and chopped
demerara sugar

Line a 22.5 cm (9 inch) flan dish with the pastry, and chill while you prepare the filling.

Mix sausagemeat with the sage in a heatproof dish and put in oven at 350°F/180°C/Gas 4 for about 15 minutes to remove excess fat. Drain this off.

Parboil the onions for a few minutes, then chop roughly. Spread them in the bottom of the chilled pastry case. Arrange sausagemeat on top and cover finally with the chopped apple, sprinkled with a little demerara sugar.

Place in a fairly hot oven – 375–400°F/190–200°C/Gas 5–6 – and cook for approximately 30–40 minutes. Serve hot or cold.

———————————————○———————————————

Peter L. Pike, MP
— MEMBER OF PARLIAMENT FOR BURNLEY —

CIDER BAKE

SERVES 4
4 pork chops
25 g (1 oz) butter
1 large onion, peeled and sliced
1 large cooking apple, peeled and sliced
1 tablespoon brown sugar
150 ml (¼ pint) cider
chicken stock if necessary
dried thyme
salt and freshly ground black pepper

Lightly fry the chops in the butter until just brown, and place them in a casserole. Fry the onion lightly in the butter remaining in the pan.

Top the chops with the onion and sliced apple. Sprinkle with brown sugar and cover with the cider (top up with chicken stock if necessary). Add thyme, salt and pepper to taste.

Cover and cook in a slow oven at about 300°F/150°C/Gas 2 for 2–3 hours.

———————————— ○ ————————————

Rt Hon Dr David Owen, MP
— Member of Parliament for Plymouth, Devonport —

LAMB KIDNEYS WITH MUSTARD SAUCE

Serves 2
40 g (1½ oz) butter
6 lamb's kidneys (can be more or less, depending on your appetite), skinned and trimmed of all fat
1 tablespoon finely chopped spring onions (or ordinary onions)
75 ml (2½ fl. oz) dry white wine
1 tablespoon Dijon mustard
salt and freshly ground black pepper
chopped parsley

Melt 25 g (1 oz) of the butter in a shallow casserole or deep frying pan and add kidneys. Cook on all sides for about 10 minutes, by which time kidneys should be cooked on the outside and pink in the centre. Remove to a warm plate.

Add onion to butter left in the casserole or pan, and cook for 1 minute. Then add the white wine and boil while scraping up the bits from the bottom of the pan. Take off the heat and mix in the mustard and remaining butter along with salt and pepper to taste.

Slice kidneys at a slight angle about 6 mm (¼ inch) thick, then add to the sauce in the pan. Put back over a low heat for a couple of minutes to heat the kidneys through. Add a sprinkling of parsley, and serve with boiled rice.

———————— ○ ————————

Rt Hon Peter Thomas, QC
— Ex Member of Parliament for Hendon South —

TRIPE AND ONIONS

A good meal can make one feel more charitable towards the world than any sermon.

Serves 4
450 g (1 lb) tripe, cut into pieces
600 ml (1 pint) milk
225 g (½ lb) onions, peeled and sliced
50 g (2 oz) butter
50 g (2 oz) plain flour
salt and freshly ground black pepper

Blanch tripe in sufficient water to cover. Drain and add milk and sliced onions. Top up with water to cover if necessary. Cover tightly and cook gently until tripe is soft, about 2 hours.

Make a roux with butter and flour. Add some liquid from the cooking tripe and onions to the roux and allow to thicken. Pour the sauce back into the saucepan with the tripe, and add pepper and salt to taste. Thicken and then serve with creamed and buttered potatoes.

———————————— o ————————————

Sam Galbraith, MP
— MEMBER OF PARLIAMENT FOR STRATHKELVIN AND BEARSDEN —

HAGGIS, TATTIES AND NEEPS

This dish can be served either as a starter or as a main course. Its great benefit is that a number of people do not like it and this means there is more for the rest of us. In order to achieve the full pleasure it is necessary to wash it down with some whisky to taste, preferably a fine malt.

Serves 6
3 haggis (standard size)
1 large turnip (swede), peeled and cut into small pieces
2.7 kg (6 lb) potatoes, peeled and cut into small pieces
butter and milk

Place the haggii in a pot and cover with water. Bring to the boil and simmer for 40 minutes. Boil turnip (neeps) and potato (tatties), separately, until soft. Mash them, separately, adding a knob of butter to both, and some milk to the potatoes.

Puncture the haggii with a large knife and serve in huge quantities.

———————————— o ————————————

POULTRY
AND
GAME DISHES

Rt Hon Margaret Thatcher, MP
— MEMBER OF PARLIAMENT FOR FINCHLEY —

SAUTÉ OF CHICKEN WITH TARRAGON SAUCE

SERVES 4
4 portions frying chicken
25 g (1 oz) butter
300 ml (½ pint) dry white wine
TARRAGON SAUCE
15 g (½ oz) butter
1 rasher bacon, rinded and finely chopped
1 small onion, peeled and finely chopped
1 tablespoon flour
300 ml (½ pint) chicken stock
2 teaspoons concentrated tomato purée
salt and freshly ground black pepper
2 tablespoons chopped fresh tarragon

Begin by making the sauce. Heat the butter in a small pan and fry the bacon and onion until just beginning to brown. Add the flour, mix in and cook until just beginning to brown. Add the chicken stock, tomato purée, salt and pepper, and stir until boiling. Leave to simmer gently while the chicken is cooked.

Wipe the chicken portions and fry in the hot butter in a deep frying pan until golden on both sides. Lower the heat, cover the pan and cook slowly for about 30 minutes or until the chicken is tender. Remove from the pan and keep warm in a low oven.

Add the tarragon to the sauce and the wine to the pan in which the chicken was cooked. Stir until the wine comes to the boil, then boil until reduced by half. Add the tarragon sauce and mix. Return the chicken pieces to the sauce and turn them over in it to coat them well. Make sure they are hot before serving with mashed potatoes.

Rt Hon Julian Amery, MP
— MEMBER OF PARLIAMENT FOR BRIGHTON, PAVILION —

ROAST CHICKEN

Take a good roasting fowl. Roast it for three-quarters of the appropriate time for cooking. Transfer it to a frying pan and pour a little less than a quarter bottle of whisky or brandy over it. Set it on fire and keep basting it with the mixture of spirits and its own juice until the flames have gone out. Add a substantial quantity of double cream and continue rotating over the fire. Place on a carving board. Carve and cover the carved portions with the juices from the frying pan.

○

Andrew MacKay, MP
— MEMBER OF PARLIAMENT FOR BERKSHIRE EAST —

TARRAGON CHICKEN

This is a very easy dish to cook and prepare, and any stuffing could easily replace the tarragon stuffing given here.

SERVES 8
8 chicken breasts
chicken stock
beurre manié (equal quantities of butter and flour mixed together), if necessary
STUFFING
3 teaspoons butter
2 tablespoons finely chopped shallot or spring onion
2 tablespoons finely chopped fresh tarragon
a bunch of watercress, finely chopped
4 tablespoons dry white wine
breadcrumbs (amount depends on size of chicken breasts)
salt and freshly ground black pepper

To make the stuffing, melt the butter and gently cook the shallot until soft. Add tarragon, watercress, white wine and breadcrumbs. Stir and cook gently for 2–3 minutes, then season to taste.

Separate skin from each chicken breast and spread stuffing between skin and flesh. Fold back skin to form a parcel. Put the stuffed breasts in a flat dish and cover with chicken stock. Cover dish and bake for 20 minutes at 350°F/180°C/Gas 4. Remove cover and cook for a further 20 minutes or so to brown the top of the chicken breasts.

Keep the chicken warm on a serving plate, and thicken the cooking juices, either by boiling to reduce, or with beurre manié, if required. Serve the chicken breasts with a little of the juices and pass the rest around separately.

———— ○ ————

Rt Hon Sir Geoffrey Howe, QC, MP
— MEMBER OF PARLIAMENT FOR SURREY EAST —

POULET EN CASSEROLE NORMANDE

SERVES 4
1 medium chicken
40 g (1½ oz) butter
1 medium onion, peeled and sliced, or 12 baby onions, peeled and left whole
2 streaky bacon rashers, rinded, cut into lardons and blanched
2 well flavoured apples, peeled, cored and cut into eighths
salt and freshly ground black pepper
approx. 150 ml (¼ pint) cider (preferably draught)
1 bouquet garni

Brown the chicken all over in the hot butter. Remove it, put the onion in pan and sauté over a moderate heat. After a few minutes, add the bacon, increase the heat, and when pan contents are turning colour, add the apples. Shake over a brisk heat briefly.

Now carve and joint the chicken nearby, and break the back into two or three pieces. Arrange the bird in a casserole in layers with the mixture from the pan, and plenty of seasoning. Rinse the pan out with the cider, which may be diluted with a little water if wished, and pour into the casserole. Tuck the bouquet garni down the side, lay the pieces of back on the top, and cover tightly, sealing round the edges, if necessary, with a flour and water paste. Cook in a slow to moderate oven (300–325°F/150–160°C/Gas 2–3) for 1½–2½ hours, according to the age of the bird.

———— ○ ————

David Menhennet
— LIBRARIAN, HOUSE OF COMMONS LIBRARY —

CHICKEN LYONESSE

This is my family's variation of a delightful main course which we ate once in a small French restaurant in Brussels, which advertised the principal feature of its menu as 'pas de frites ici'! The dish was described as 'Escalope de Dindon Normande' and this recipe is based on it. We have named it 'Chicken Lyonesse' to remind us of a time when Cornwall and France were supposedly linked.

SERVES 4
450 g (1 lb) chicken or turkey breasts (or white flesh pieces)
25 g (1 oz) butter
1 medium leek, cleaned and sliced
2 medium cooking or dessert apples, peeled, cored and chopped
100 g (¼ lb) mushrooms, washed and sliced
1 tablespoon plain flour
300 ml (½ pint) chicken stock
1 full wine glass West Country cider, or sherry
salt and freshly ground black pepper to taste
2 tablespoons cream
1 teaspoon fresh chopped parsley

Fry the chicken or turkey pieces in butter in a saucepan for a few minutes until brown. Remove from pan and place in a casserole. Fry the leek, apple and mushroom in butter remaining in pan. Remove when light brown and add to the casserole.

Blend flour and stock in pan, stirring well into remaining butter. Add cider or sherry, and season to taste. Cook for a few minutes then pour the sauce into the casserole over the other ingredients.

Place in the oven and cook at 325°F/160°C/Gas 3 for 1 hour. (This dish may be cooked for a little longer than an hour, or it can be reheated.)

Add the cream and chopped parsley just before serving with, if you like, mashed potatoes, spinach or sweetcorn.

———————————— ○ ————————————

Rt Hon Sir Bernard Braine, DL, MP
— Member of Parliament for Castle Point, Father of the House —

Bernard Braine

CHICKEN FRUIT CURRY

A meal not to be interrupted by division bells but to be shared with friends and eaten in a leisurely fashion by candlelight.

SERVES 4
4 chicken breasts, skinned
40 g (1½ oz) butter
1 level tablespoon curry powder
1 teaspoon curry paste or garam masala
1 medium onion, peeled and finely chopped
a small piece fresh green ginger, or 25 g (1 oz) ground ginger
salt
75 ml (2½ fl. oz) chicken stock
1 tablespoon redcurrant jelly
pineapple slices, halved
stoned plums
sliced peaches
75 ml (2½ fl. oz) cream (optional)

Fresh fruit is best, but you can use canned.

Brown the chicken pieces in the butter in a lidded frying pan, and then add the curry powder and paste (or garam masala) with the onion. Cook for 2–3 minutes, then add the ginger. Salt lightly, then pour in the chicken stock. Cover tightly and simmer gently for 20 minutes. Take out the chicken pieces, arrange in a serving dish, and keep warm.

Add the redcurrant jelly to the pan and when dissolved, add the fruit (as little or as much as you like). Cover and poach until the fruit is tender.

Lift the fruit carefully on to the chicken, spooning the juices over as well. You can, if desired, add the cream to the juices in the pan. Bring to the boil and strain over the chicken.

Serve with rice and 'sambals'.

———————————○———————————

Paul Boateng, MP
— MEMBER OF PARLIAMENT FOR BRENT SOUTH —

Paul Boateng

HKATENKWAN (Groundnut or Peanut Stew)

This recipe comes from Ghana. If you wish to serve it as a soup, use 6 or more cups of water to cook the chicken.

SERVES 4–6

1 chicken, cut into pieces	²⁄₃ cup peanut butter
1 × 2.5 cm (1 inch) piece fresh root ginger	2 teaspoons salt
½ onion, peeled	2 hot chillies, crushed, or 1 teaspoon
2 tablespoons tomato paste	cayenne pepper (to taste)
1 tablespoon peanut oil	1 medium aubergine, peeled and cubed
1 cup finely chopped onion	(optional)
1 cup chopped tomatoes	2 cups fresh or frozen okra (optional)

Boil chicken in a pot with ginger, onion half and 2 cups water. Meanwhile, in a separate large pot, fry tomato paste in the oil over low heat for about 5 minutes. Add chopped onion and tomato and cook, stirring occasionally, until the onions are transparent.

Remove the partially cooked chicken pieces and put them, along with about half the stock, in the large pot. Add the peanut butter, salt and chillies or cayenne. Cook for 5 minutes before stirring in the aubergine and okra (if used). Continue cooking until chicken and vegetables are tender. Add more stock as needed for a thick, stewy consistency.

———————————— ○ ————————————

Peter Griffiths, MP
— MEMBER OF PARLIAMENT FOR PORTSMOUTH NORTH —

Peter Griffiths

CHICKEN BREASTS VÉRONIQUE

This recipe comes from California where my grape-grower friends are always looking to increase their sales. In this case they have a winner even if we usually use Cyprus grapes.

4 chicken breasts, skinned and boned
salt
25 g (1 oz) butter
1½ tablespoons orange marmalade
½ teaspoon dried tarragon leaves, crumbled
125 ml (4 fl. oz) dry white wine
125 ml (4 fl. oz) whipping cream
2 teaspoons cornflour mixed with a little water
about 100 g (¼ lb) seedless grapes

Cut the chicken breasts in half and sprinkle lightly with salt. Melt the butter in a wide frying pan over medium heat. Add the breasts and brown lightly on each side.

Blend the marmalade, tarragon and wine, and pour into the pan. Stir together, then cover and simmer very gently for about 20 minutes, or until the thickest section of the breasts is white in the centre. Transfer the breasts to a serving dish and keep hot.

Add the cream to the pan juices and quickly bring to a rolling boil. Stir the cornflour mixture into the sauce, and return to the boil, stirring. Add the grapes, return to the boil, and immediately pour over the chicken.

———————————————— o ————————————————

David Madel, MP
— MEMBER OF PARLIAMENT FOR BEDFORDSHIRE SOUTH WEST —

David Madel

CHICKEN SALAD

SERVES 4

1 dessertspoon lemon juice
3 tablespoons mayonnaise
salt and freshly ground black pepper
450 g (1 lb) cold cooked chicken, chopped
225 g (½ lb) mushrooms, sliced

1 red pepper, seeded and diced
½ cucumber, chopped
chopped fresh parsley
50 g (2 oz) flaked almonds, toasted

Stir lemon juice into mayonnaise and season to taste with salt and pepper. Add chopped chicken, mushrooms, red pepper and cucumber. Mix together gently, then sprinkle with chopped parsley and flaked toasted almonds.

———————————————— o ————————————————

Keith Vaz, MP
— Member of Parliament for Leicester East —

Keith Vaz

Leicester East Chicken (Gur ka Murghi)

My idea of a meal is having absolutely nothing to do with its preparation. However, I enjoy eating. This dish is my steady standby and I bestow it on the nation with pleasure. Happy eating.

Serves 4–6
6 pieces chicken (preferably thighs), skinned
1 tablespoon oil
1 onion, peeled and finely sliced
1 tomato, sliced
1 tablespoon honey mixed with ½ teaspoon chilli powder
1 tablespoon garam masala (can be bought in any supermarket)
1 tea cup natural yoghurt
salt and freshly ground black pepper
a few sprigs of fresh coriander (optional)

Wash the chicken pieces and pat dry with a paper towel. Fry in the hot oil, turning them frequently. Drain and place in an ovenproof dish.

Fry the onion, tomato, honey and chilli mixture. Add the garam masala and stir in the yoghurt. Stir well and draw off the heat if the mixture begins to stick. Pour this over the chicken pieces. Add salt and pepper to taste, and sprinkle with the coriander if used. Put on the lid and bake for 1 hour in the preheated oven at 375°F/190°C/Gas 5.

———————— ○ ————————

Michael Howard, QC, MP

— MEMBER OF PARLIAMENT FOR FOLKESTONE AND HYTHE —

DUCK WITH WILD RICE STUFFING

SERVES 4
1 large (1.8–2.25 kg/4–5 lb) duck
salt and freshly ground black pepper
1 garlic clove, peeled
STUFFING
50 g (2 oz) butter
3 tablespoons chopped celery
3 small onions, peeled and chopped
175 g (6 oz) cooked wild rice
2 teaspoons curry powder
ORANGE SAUCE
2 tablespoons thinly pared, finely sliced, strips of orange peel
300 ml (½ pint) orange juice
1 glass wine (red or white)
2 tablespoons redcurrant jelly
a scant teaspoon Dijon mustard
a pinch of cayenne pepper
a handful of pith-free orange segments

Prick the skin of the duck all over with a fork. Season and rub with the cut garlic clove. Roast in a hot oven – 425°F/220°C/Gas 7 – for 20 minutes, and then strain off the fat.

Meanwhile make the stuffing. Melt the butter and blend with all the other ingredients, adding 2 teaspoons salt and some pepper.

When the duck is cool enough to handle, stuff it with the stuffing. Return to the oven, reduced to medium – 350°F/180°C/Gas 4 – and cook for about 1½ hours.

Meanwhile, start the orange sauce. Simmer the orange peel and juice together for 20 minutes very gently. When the duck is cooked, remove from the roasting pan and put on a platter. Keep warm. Strain the fat from the pan, and pour in the orange peel and juice plus all the remaining sauce ingredients – except for the orange segments. Add some salt to taste. Stir to mix in the tasty stuck remains from the pan, and cook until the jelly has melted. Add the orange segments and serve.

John Watts, MP
— MEMBER OF PARLIAMENT FOR SLOUGH —

PAELLA

Paella is a dish of manifold attractions. It is flexible and adaptable to personal tastes. As the entire meal is cooked in one pan, the burden of washing up is light. The enjoyment of so many delightful dishes is ruined by the contemplation of a sinkful of sticky saucepans awaiting the ministrations of a scourer.

I prefer a wok to cook my paella, but a large cast-iron frying pan will do equally well. But it must be large.

Heat a little oil in the pan and fry a finely chopped onion or two with the lid on until the onion is soft. Meanwhile joint a chicken into about ten pieces. Skin the chicken (unless you are partial to crisp chicken skin, in which case you can remove the skin during the cooking and eat it to stave off the pangs of hunger).

Add the chicken to the onion and cook gently with the lid on, turning from time to time, until it is cooked through. Move the chicken and onion to the outside of the pan and add a cup of rice. Fry gently but do not allow the rice to burn.

Add a chicken stock cube and crushed garlic or garlic granules (to taste) to some boiling chicken stock or boiling water. If using dried peppers they can be added at this stage. Add the stock to the pan and stir the rice thoroughly. The entire contents of the pan should be covered by the stock.

Add frozen peas, mixed peppers, mushrooms, mussels (preferably in their shells), prawns (or lobster if you are feeling affluent). Keep the pan covered until the stock comes back to the boil. Uncover and keep boiling gently until most of the liquid has been absorbed by the rice or has evaporated, stirring occasionally to ensure the rice does not stick.

If you have cooked too much there is no need to worry. This dish freezes well and can be reheated successfully in a microwave oven or in a saucepan with added boiling water.

———————— ○ ————————

Sir John Biggs-Davison, MP
— Member of Parliament for Epping Forest —

John Biggs-Davison

Normandy Pheasant

Not Harold's Revenge. 'Pheasant' **not** 'Peasant'.

Serves 4
2 plump pheasants, cleaned and trussed
50 g (2 oz) butter
2 large tart apples, peeled and sliced
1 wine glass Calvados (or brandy)
300 ml (½ pint) double cream
juice of ½ lemon
salt and freshly ground black pepper

Sauté the pheasants in half the butter in a heavy-bottomed frying pan until brown on all sides. Keep warm.

Sauté the sliced apples in the remaining butter in the same pan. Arrange the slices in the bottom of an earthenware casserole and place the pheasants on top.

Thin the juices left in the frying pan with Calvados (or brandy), and pour this liquid over the birds. Place in the preheated oven at 375°F/190°C/Gas 5 and roast, uncovered, for 30 minutes, basting occasionally.

Add cream and lemon juice, stirring them into the cooking juices, and season with salt and pepper. Return to the oven, covered, for another 1–1½ hours, until the birds are tender and the sauce is rich and creamy.

Serve with game chips, and pear halves stuffed with chestnut purée which have been slightly steamed in a pan with a little butter.

———————— ○ ————————

Fred Silvester
— Ex Member of Parliament for Manchester, Withington —

Fred Silvester

Turkey Blanquette

Serves 4
2 tablespoons oil
450 g (1 lb) turkey breast, cubed
225 g (½ lb) button mushrooms, sliced
6–8 small onions, peeled
3 tablespoons plain flour
150 ml (¼ pint) white wine
150 ml (¼ pint) chicken stock
1–2 tablespoons chopped fresh parsley
2 tablespoons capers
salt and freshly ground black pepper
2 tablespoons soured fresh cream

In a microwave
Put a microwave bag in a large glass or pottery mixing bowl. On a conventional hob, heat oil in a saucepan, stir in turkey and cook for 5 minutes, stirring occasionally. Add mushroom and onion and cook for 2 minutes. Stir in flour and cook for a minute. Gradually stir in wine and stock then bring to the boil, stirring. Stir in parsley, capers and seasoning. Remove from heat and stir in cream. Spoon into bag. Close bag loosely with twist-tie provided. Microwave on *full power* for 8 minutes.

In a conventional oven
Put microwave bag in a large casserole, then prepare as above. Make six small slits in the bag. Cook in a preheated oven at 350°F/180°C/Gas 4 for 45 minutes.

To freeze
Cool, transfer bag to a rigid container, tighten twist-tie then freeze quickly until solid. Label.

To serve
Loosen twist-tie. Microwave on *defrost* for 20 minutes, then on *roast* for 17 minutes, stirring halfway through cooking. In a conventional oven, return frozen bag to casserole, loosen twist-tie and reheat in a preheated oven at 400°F/200°C/Gas 6 for 1 hour, stirring after 40 minutes.

Robert Key, MP
— MEMBER OF PARLIAMENT FOR SALISBURY —

Robert Key

Delectable vegetarian dishes have their place but hare and venison are as traditional as poaching, were for centuries staple food, and have the extra virtue of being quite delicious.

MOONRAKER HARE

Hang the hare for 10 days then skin, clean and joint. Marinade in vinegar and water, olive oil, juniper berries, pepper, shallots, garlic, salt, bay leaves and carrots, for at least 12 hours.

Casserole slowly for about 2 hours in red wine, a dash of brandy, with mushrooms, diced bacon and tomato purée. Serve with turnips and red cabbage.

HAUNCH OF WILTSHIRE VENISON

Good venison from a country butcher is very good value – compares favourably with lamb. Ensure the joint – of about 1.8 kg (4 lb) – is well hung (about a week). Remove the membrane.

Make a marinade by sweating onions, carrots and celery in goose fat. Add water and vinegar or red wine, with salt, peppercorns, allspice, bay leaves and thyme. Simmer for half an hour and allow to cool.

Marinate the joint for at least 12 hours.

Remove it, dry it, baste liberally with goose fat (or butter). Roast for about 2 hours at 375°F/190°C/Gas 5, keeping the venison moist with marinade. Slice thickly and serve with sloe jelly.

E. J. Nash

— DEPUTY GENERAL MANAGER, REFRESHMENT DEPARTMENT, HOUSE OF COMMONS —

Nash.

EDDIE'S PHEASANT WITH CRANBERRIES AND GINGER WINE SAUCE

PER PERSON
1 raw pheasant breast
25 g (1 oz) plain flour
salt and freshly ground black pepper
50 g (2 oz) butter
1 small shallot, peeled and finely chopped
50 ml (2 fl. oz) ginger wine
8 black peppercorns, crushed
50 ml (2 fl. oz) double cream
½ teaspoon chopped fresh tarragon
25 g (1 oz) cranberries, fresh or frozen
toasted or fried bread croûtons, edges dipped in finely chopped parsley

Dip both sides of the pheasant breast in the flour seasoned with a little salt and pepper, and shake off the excess.

Heat the butter in a heavy pan until it starts to brown, then cook the pheasant breast for 5 minutes on each side. Remove pheasant from the pan and keep warm.

Add the shallot to the butter left in the pan and cook until golden brown. Add ginger wine and the peppercorns and mix well with a wooden spoon.

Then add the cream, tarragon, cranberries and the pheasant breast and bring to the boil. Place the pheasant breast on a warmed serving plate and cover with the sauce.

Place the fried croûtons on top and serve immediately.

———————————— ○ ————————————

Hon Robert Boscawen, MC, MP
— Member of Parliament for Somerton and Frome —

Robert Boscawen

Casserole of Pheasant or Grouse

Serves 4
1 large pheasant or 2 grouse
25 g (1 oz) butter
1 tablespoon oil
1 large onion, peeled and sliced
50 g (2 oz) plain flour
600 ml (1 pint) stock
juice and finely grated rind of 1 orange
1 tablespoon redcurrant jelly
150 ml (¼ pint) port
1 bay leaf
1 parsley sprig
salt and freshly ground black pepper

Cut the pheasant into four portions, or cut each grouse in half. Heat the butter and oil in a pan and quickly fry the birds on all sides until a golden colour. Remove from the pan and place in a casserole.

Add the onion to the butter and oil remaining in the pan and cook until soft. Stir in the flour and cook, stirring, for about 5 minutes, or until golden brown. Gradually add the stock and bring to the boil, stirring all the time. Allow to thicken and then add the remaining ingredients. Pour over the pheasant or grouse in the casserole.

Cover and cook in a warm oven at 325°F/160°C/Gas 3 for 2–4 hours, depending on the age of the birds. Taste and adjust the seasoning before serving.

———————————— ○ ————————————

William Benyon, MP for Milton Keynes, offers an interesting recipe for Englefield Game Pie, which has 'certainly been in use for 150 years'. Part-cook a skinned and boned hare, 900 g (2 lb) sausagemeat, 225 g (½ lb) streaky bacon and boned legs of 2 pheasants in a little oil. Season and put through mincer. Line a casserole dish with some of this mixture, top with the pheasant breasts in strips, then cover with the remaining mixture. Cook in a bain-marie in the oven at 300°F/150°C/Gas 2 for 2½ hours. When cold, pour aspic over the top.

Egg, Cheese
AND
Vegetable Dishes

K. S. Morgan
— EDITOR, OFFICIAL REPORT (HANSARD) —

HANSARD OMELETTE

Serves four to six ordinary people or one Hansard Editor after an all-nighter.

25–50 g (1–2 oz) fat
1 × 200 g (7 oz) can English chopped ham with pork, thickly sliced
1 teaspoon potato flour or cornflour
8 tablespoons milk
6 eggs, beaten
salt and freshly ground black pepper
2 tomatoes, thickly sliced
snipped chives

Heat fat in a frying pan, and fry the ham slices for 2 minutes, turning over once.

Mix the potato flour or cornflour to a paste with a little of the milk in a large bowl, then mix in the remaining milk, the beaten eggs, a little salt and some pepper. Pour over the ham in the frying pan and cook gently over medium heat for 5 minutes. Add the sliced tomatoes and snipped chives and cook for a further 3 minutes.

Loosen edges of omelette with a knife, slide on to a plate (or plates), and serve hot with mustard.

———————————— ○ ————————————

Dr Charles Goodson-Wickes, MP for Wimbledon, recommends Artichokes Lionheart: 'Edible thistles they may be, but these artichokes formed part of the first civilized lunch after 4 weeks of campaigning.' Warm the contents of a can of artichoke hearts, and make a cheese sauce. Add some of the can juices to the sauce, along with a little Worcestershire sauce and a dash of Tabasco, and pour over the hearts. Serve hot with garlic bread.

Richard Needham, MP
— MEMBER OF PARLIAMENT FOR WILTSHIRE NORTH —

INDA'S EGG

This is a dish I first came across in Northern Ireland.

SERVES 5–6
12 hard-boiled eggs, sliced
butter
3 tablespoons flour
600 ml (1 pint) milk
3 large onions, peeled and sliced
225 g (½ lb) (tasty) Cheddar cheese, grated

With 65 g (2½ oz) of the butter, plus the flour and the milk, make a white sauce to a medium thick consistency. Fry the sliced onions in a little more butter until transparent but not brown.

Grease an ovenproof dish with butter and layer alternately with the fried onions and sliced boiled eggs. Cover with the sauce. Repeat. Cover with grated cheese and brown under grill or in oven. If liked some of the cheese can be added to the sauce.

Can be served as a starter or as a snack with hot brown rolls and salad.

———————— o ————————

Ian Stewart, RD, MP
— MEMBER OF PARLIAMENT FOR HERTFORDSHIRE NORTH —

OEUFS À LA STEWART

mushrooms
red wine if possible
ham or any suitable meat
parsley
eggs (2 plus per person)

milk
salt
red pepper
butter if necessary

Peel the mushrooms and dice very small; simmer very gently on a low gas in a large frying pan for at least 15 minutes, preferably in red wine, otherwise in stock (fat should not be used, if possible, and in any case only dripping).

Meanwhile, cut up about 100 g (¼ lb) of ham or cold meat very fine, and chop at least 20 g (¾ oz) of parsley with it. Also, beat the eggs, adding a little milk (not cream), 3 pinches of salt and a little red pepper.

When the mushrooms are ready, strain off the wine or stock and add a little butter (if dripping is used this is not necessary); keep the gas very low and when the mushrooms are frying slowly in the melted butter add the parsley and ham; then pour on the eggs.

The fat in the pan should be just enough to allow the contents to cook without sticking to the pan.

When the egg is beginning to thicken as for an omelette, turn up the gas, and cook quickly for about a minute by stirring with a spoon as for scrambled eggs.

Serve on hot buttered toast. For three people use about 7 eggs, 100 g (¼ lb) mushrooms and 100 g (¼ lb) ham.

———————————————○———————————————

Charles Irving, MP
— MEMBER OF PARLIAMENT FOR CHELTENHAM —

CHELTENHAM CHEESE PUDDING

SERVES 3–4
175 g (6 oz) Cheddar, Cheshire or Lancashire cheese, grated
2 eggs
300 ml (½ pint) milk
freshly ground black pepper

Put the cheese in a buttered oval ovenproof dish.

Beat the eggs and milk together with lots of pepper, pour over the cheese and bake in a preheated oven at 350°F/180°C/Gas 4 for 30 minutes. Serve immediately.

Mrs Elizabeth J. Peacock, JP, MP
— MEMBER OF PARLIAMENT FOR BATLEY AND SPEN —

CHEESE SOUFFLÉ

25 g (1 oz) butter
30–35 g (1¼ oz) plain flour
300 ml (½ pint) milk
75 g (3 oz) Cheddar cheese, grated
2 eggs, separated
salt and freshly ground black pepper
mustard powder
25 g (1 oz) peeled prawns (if desired)

Grease a soufflé dish well. Melt butter in a pan, add flour and mix well. Cook over gentle heat for 1 minute. Take off heat, and add the milk slowly. Return to heat and bring to the boil, stirring continuously. Remove from heat, and add cheese and egg yolks. Season to taste with salt, pepper and a little mustard powder. Add prawns if required.

Beat egg whites stiffly, and fold lightly into mixture with a metal spoon. Put into dish and into the well preheated oven at 400°F/200°C/Gas 6 for about 35 minutes. Serve immediately.

———————○———————

Rt Hon David Steel, MP
— MEMBER OF PARLIAMENT FOR TWEEDDALE, ETTRICK AND LAUDERDALE —

David Steel

WELSH RAREBIT

225 g (½ lb) fresh Cheddar or Cheshire cheese
½ tsp mustard powder
a little paprika
a few grains of cayenne pepper
salt
a little beer or stout
hot buttered toast

Shred the cheese and put it in a double boiler. Let it melt slowly over hot water kept just under boiling point. Add the mustard, paprika and cayenne, and salt to taste, according to the needs of the cheese. Then stir in gradually as much beer as the cheese will absorb. The mixture should be smooth and velvety.

Serve on hot buttered toast or hot toasted biscuits.

———————○———————

Rt Hon Nicholas Edwards
— Ex Member of Parliament for Pembroke —

Welsh Leeks

Allow 2 medium-sized leeks per head. Wash leeks by slitting lengthways to within an inch of the base. Rinse grit out by running under a cold tap. They can be cooked in three different ways.

Chop across in 3.75 cm (1½ inch) lengths. Boil in salted water for 10 minutes or until tender. Drain into colander and leave dry cloth on top to steam. Make a rich white sauce with the addition of double cream and a pinch of nutmeg. Place leeks in a warm dish and pour sauce over.

Leave leeks whole after washing. Boil in salted water for 5 minutes. Drain. Lay leeks in a flat ovenproof dish. Dot with butter, salt and freshly ground black pepper. Roast in medium oven for approximately 40 minutes on the middle shelf or below the roast until leeks are slightly brown and crispy.

As above, but after dotting the leeks with butter, salt and pepper, grate a hard cheese such as Caerphilly all over the top and roast the same way until cheese is golden brown. This is an adequate supper snack on its own served with hot brown rolls and salad.

———————————————— o ————————————————

Alan Meale, MP
— Member of Parliament for Mansfield —

Leek Pudding

Being born and raised in a County Durham mining village I learned to be in awe of this dish, especially as the leeks used were those grown every year for prize showing in the County's villages throughout the month of September. The leeks themselves are at least ten times their normal size due to individual care and specialist (sometimes secret) feeding programmes.

900 g (2 lb) leeks, washed and finely chopped
300 g (10 oz) plain flour
salt and freshly ground black pepper

100 g (¼ lb) shredded suet
2 eggs
½ cup milk

Combine the flour, seasoning and suet in a mixing bowl and make a well in the centre. In another bowl beat the eggs and milk. Pour into the dry ingredients and mix thoroughly, adding more milk if necessary to obtain an easy dropping consistency.

Add the washed and finely chopped leeks to the mix and stir thoroughly. Turn into well greased pudding basins and cover with greaseproof paper. Bake in a hot oven – preheated to about 425–450°F/220–230°C/Gas 7–8 – for 45–60 minutes until pudding is dry on the top. Turn out on to a serving dish and surround with fresh cooked carrots and new potatoes. Pour a light but well seasoned beef gravy over the pudding, and cut to serve.

———————— o ————————

Anthony Hodges
— *The Times* —

POTATO BAKE

This comes from a cookery book compiled by a cousin of mine of recipes from members of my family, now scattered around the world.

SERVES 4

4 medium potatoes, peeled
2 medium onions, peeled
100 g (¼ lb) Cheddar cheese, grated

chopped parsley
4 streaky bacon rashers
a few knobs of butter

Slice potatoes so that they are about 6 mm (¼ inch) thick. Cut onions into rings.

Using an ovenproof dish, start with the potatoes and make layers of potato, then onion, sprinkling the grated cheese and chopped parsley on top. When everything is used up, place the bacon rashers over the top and add a few knobs of butter.

Cover the dish and bake at the top of a preheated oven – 375°F/190°C/Gas 5 – for 30 minutes. Remove the lid and cook, uncovered, for a further 30 minutes.

———————— o ————————

Miss Joan Maynard, JP
— Ex Member of Parliament for Sheffield, Brightside —

Joan Maynard.

CAULIFLOWER CHEESE SPECIAL

Serves 4
1 medium cauliflower, separated into large florets
100 g (¼ lb) button mushrooms, sliced
some chopped red and green peppers
1 medium carrot, scrubbed and grated
25 g (1 oz) butter
3 hard-boiled eggs
450 ml (¾ pint) white sauce
175 g (6 oz) Cheddar cheese, grated

Cook cauliflower until barely tender (do not *overcook*).

Sauté mushrooms, peppers and carrot in the butter for a few minutes.

Cut the hard-boiled eggs in half and lay in the bottom of a dish with the sautéed veg. Then put cauliflower in on top. Make the white sauce as usual and put in most of the cheese. Pour over cauliflower and sprinkle top with remaining cheese. Grill until a light golden colour.

If a more substantial dish is required, cook 100 g (¼ lb) of pasta shells and put in bottom of dish.

Serve with a green side salad.

Rt Hon John Stanley, MP
— Member of Parliament for Tonbridge and Malling —

SPINACH AND GARLIC ROULADE

Votes taken in my family have produced a tie between Spinach and Garlic Roulade, favoured by the girls as a light luncheon dish, and Bread and Butter Pudding, which has the particular approval of the male members of the family. The girls have been allowed to carry the day.

Serves 4
450 g (1 lb) fresh spinach
5 eggs, separated
salt and freshly ground black pepper
1 teaspoon finely grated lemon rind
a little grated nutmeg
4 tablespoons grated Parmesan cheese
2 × 75 g (2¾ oz) packets Boursin cheese with garlic and herbs
1–2 tablespoons double cream

Line and grease a 32.5 × 22.5 cm (13 × 9 inch) Swiss roll tin.

Wash the spinach well, shake off excess water, and cook in its own juices until just tender. Drain, then chop or liquidize – but not too finely. Beat spinach with egg yolks, salt and pepper, lemon rind, nutmeg and most of the grated Parmesan.

Whisk the egg whites until they form soft peaks, and fold lightly into the spinach mixture.

Fill prepared tin evenly with mixture and bake at 350°F/180°C/Gas 4 for about 20 minutes, until firm but still spongy.

Remove from tin and carefully peel off the paper. Mix the cheese well with the cream and spread over the roulade. Roll up and sprinkle with the remaining Parmesan cheese. Return to the oven for 5 minutes then serve immediately.

———————— ○ ————————

Rt Hon Michael Jopling, MP
— MEMBER OF PARLIAMENT FOR WESTMORLAND AND LONSDALE —

BAKED SAVOURY POTATO

When I first got married, an old man told me: 'First, never tell your wife how much money you have. Second, whatever she asks you to do in the house, do it; but do it badly.'

Take a large potato, preferably grown in Yorkshire. Place it in a hot oven until it is cooked. Split it in two and cut out a hollow in each half. Fill with as much butter and either Bovril or Marmite as it is possible to get in. Then eat.

This is one of the world's great tastes.

———— o ————

Peter Bottomley, MP
— MEMBER OF PARLIAMENT FOR ELTHAM —

BOTTOMLEY POTATO PIES

These kept me going during my vegetarian youth. Instead of a nightly battle with my mother about eating meat, aged eleven I went to the United States on the Queen Elizabeth. Claiming immunity from meat in international waters, I was given permission to eat what *I* wanted. I had five puddings for breakfast, lunch and tea. There was never a happier eleven year old.

Bake potatoes.

Cut in half, scrape out the middles and mix with butter or margarine, cheese, season to taste.

Put the mixture back into the potato jackets and grill.

———— o ————

Sir Marcus Fox, MBE, MP
— MEMBER OF PARLIAMENT FOR SHIPLEY —

CASHEW NUT ROAST WITH SULTANA STUFFING

SERVES 4
25 g (1 oz) rice flakes
1 cup water
50 g (2 oz) finely chopped leek
3 large tomatoes
oil
50 g (2 oz) cashew nuts, ground
50 g (2 oz) grated carrot
1 teaspoon dried marjoram
salt and freshly ground black pepper
50 g (2 oz) Cheddar cheese, grated
SULTANA STUFFING
25 g (1 oz) finely chopped parsnip
25 g (1 oz) finely chopped celery
25 g (1 oz) sultanas
a pinch each of ground ginger and dried mixed herbs
½ teaspoon yeast extract
GARNISH
watercress sprigs

To make the nut roast, stir rice flakes and water together in a pan, and just bring to the boil. Cook leek and 1 tomato, skinned and chopped, in a little oil, then add to rice flakes and water, along with the ground cashews, carrot, marjoram and seasonings. Mix well and place half of the mixture in a greased baking dish.

To make the stuffing, bring the parsnip and celery to the boil in a minimum of water, cook until soft and then drain. Mix in the remaining ingredients. If too dry, add a little milk or drained-off water.

Place stuffing mixture on top of the mixture in the baking dish and the other half of the nut roast mixture on top of that. Top with grated cheese and the remaining tomatoes, sliced, and bake in a moderate oven – about 350°F/180°C/Gas 4 – for 40 minutes. When cooked decorate with watercress sprigs.

———————— ○ ————————

Rt Hon Bernard Weatherill, MP
— MEMBER OF PARLIAMENT FOR CROYDON NORTH EAST —

NUT ROAST

Although I am the only vegetarian in the family it would be unthinkable for all of them to have their meat without sampling the nut roast too. They call this 'having the best of both worlds'!

SERVES ABOUT 4

1 medium onion, peeled and chopped
2 carrots, peeled and grated
2 celery sticks, finely chopped
25 g (1 oz) margarine
100 g (¼ lb) breadcrumbs
100 g (¼ lb) hazelnuts
50 g (2 oz) walnuts
1 tablespoon tomato ketchup

1 teaspoon Worcestershire sauce
a few drops of Tabasco
1 teaspoon curry powder
1 teaspoon mixed dried herbs
1 egg
salt and freshly ground black pepper
water as necessary

Sweat the onion, carrot and celery in the margarine until tender. Place in a mixer together with all the other ingredients and blend to a dropping consistency.

Place in a well greased bread tin, and bake in a medium hot oven – about 375°F/190°C/Gas 5 – for 1 hour.

———————————— ○ ————————————

Paddy Ashdown, MP
— MEMBER OF PARLIAMENT FOR YEOVIL —

LENTIL BURGERS

These are good hot or cold, in a bun with salad. Teenagers eat them 'in passing', and they're wonderful if you have vegetarians around.

225 g (½ lb) red lentils
50 g (2 oz) tasty Cheddar cheese, grated
salt and freshly ground black pepper
a handful of chopped parsley
1 egg, beaten
100 g (¼ lb) fresh brown breadcrumbs
oil for frying

Cook the lentils in water until tender, drain and then whisk them into a purée while still hot. Add the cheese, salt and pepper and allow to get cold. Add the parsley.

Fashion this 'mush' into cakes then roll in beaten egg and breadcrumbs and fry until golden brown.

———————————— ○ ————————————

Tony Speller, MP
— MEMBER OF PARLIAMENT FOR DEVON NORTH —

Tony Speller

PARSLEY PIE

This is an old West of England recipe, contributed by Mrs D. Butler.

SERVES 4–6
225 g (½ lb) shortcrust pastry
2 good handfuls fresh parsley, washed and chopped
4 bacon rashers, rinded and chopped
4 eggs
salt and freshly ground black pepper
beaten egg or milk to glaze

Roll out two-thirds of the pastry and use to line a 17.5 cm (7 inch) sandwich tin.

Sprinkle in half the parsley and cover with chopped bacon. Break eggs evenly into the pie, leaving whole, and season well. Finish with a layer of the remaining parsley.

Roll out the remaining pastry to cover the pie, damp edges and press together. Brush surface with a little beaten egg or milk, and make a small cut in the centre for steam to escape.

Bake in the preheated oven at 400°F/200°C/Gas 6 for 30–40 minutes until cooked through.

———————————— ○ ————————————

Gerald Howarth, MP
— MEMBER OF PARLIAMENT FOR CANNOCK AND BURNTWOOD —

BACHELOR's/MP's FOOD IN THE HOLE

SERVES 1–2
15 g (½ oz) lard
50 g (2 oz) bacon, rinded and chopped
1 small onion, peeled and chopped
1 tomato, sliced

BATTER
50 g (2 oz) plain flour
1 egg, size 3
4 tablespoons milk
4 tablespoons water

Put the lard into a 600 ml (1 pint) ovenproof dish, add the bacon and onion and cook in a hot oven at 450°F/230°C/Gas 8 for 15 minutes.

Meanwhile make the batter. Sift flour into a bowl, and break in the egg. Beat the egg into the flour, gradually adding the milk and water to make a smooth batter. Arrange the tomato over the bacon and onion and pour over the batter. Return to the oven and cook for 20–25 minutes, until batter is risen and golden. Serve at once.

———————————— ○ ————————————

Richard S. Wainwright, FCA
— EX MEMBER OF PARLIAMENT FOR THE COLNE VALLEY —

YORKSHIRE PUDDING

A total Yorkshireman by descent and residence. Genuine Yorkshire pudding, properly served as the first course, is a potent weapon for feminine domination of the household. For it must be eaten as soon as served; and the timing rests with Mum!

100 g (¼ lb) plain flour
a pinch of salt
1 egg
150 ml (¼ pint) ½ milk, ½ water
dripping

Yorkshire pudding should be eaten as a separate dish with a good gravy. It's best cooked in shallow Yorkshire pudding tins of about 15 cm (6 inches) in diameter (one per person), and this quantity will serve four to six people.

Sieve the flour and salt into a bowl then crack in the egg. Add the liquid gradually, beating with a wooden spoon to the consistency of thick cream. Meanwhile melt the dripping – 1 teaspoon per individual tin – until smoking hot in a preheated very hot oven (450–475°F/230–240°C/Gas 8–9). Add the pudding mixture and bake for about 10 minutes, until crisp and brown on the outside and slightly liquid in the middle.

The separate puddings should be served very promptly, with ample gravy and a knob of butter.

Stanley Crowther, MP for Rotherham, suggests adding some finely chopped onion or herbs to the batter – 'I find chives and oregano particularly acceptable.'

———————————————— ○ ————————————————

Andrew Faulds, MP
— MEMBER OF PARLIAMENT FOR WARLEY EAST —

LEEK PASTY

SERVES 4–6
450 g (1 lb) leeks, washed
450 g (1 lb) shortcrust pastry
225 g (½ lb) ham or bacon, cut into small pieces
2 eggs
4 tablespoons milk
salt and freshly ground black pepper

Cut leeks into 2.5 cm (1 inch) lengths and blanch in boiling water for 5 minutes (or microwave for 2 minutes). Leave to drain thoroughly.

Roll out the pastry. Put aside one-third for covering the pasty. Line a greased baking tin with the remainder. Put the bacon or ham in a layer on the pastry base. Add the drained leeks. Beat the eggs and the milk together and pour over the leeks. Season well.

Roll out the rest of the pastry to form a lid for the pasty, sealing the edges well. Brush with extra milk or beaten egg. Cook in a preheated oven at 350°F/180°C/Gas 4 until the pasty is brown and cooked through, about 20–30 minutes.

———————————————— ○ ————————————————

Desserts

Tim Rathbone, MP
— Member of Parliament for Lewes —

[signature: Tim Rathbone]

Khoshaf (Dried Fruit Salad)

Prepare a large quantity in advance – a day or so ahead. It gets better each day.

Serves 6
450 g (1 lb) dried apricots
225 g (½ lb) dried prunes (preferably stoned)
225 g (½ lb) seedless raisins or sultanas
100 g (¼ lb) almonds, blanched and halved
50 g (2 oz) pistachio or pine nuts, halved
175 g (6 oz) sugar or honey to taste
2 tablespoons rosewater or orange-blossom water

Wash fruit as necessary, and put in a large bowl with the other ingredients. Add water to cover, then stir and cover. Put in refrigerator or larder for 1–2 days.
Serve chilled, with whipped cream, honey and vanilla, or Greek yoghurt.

———————— ○ ————————

Rt Hon Mrs Sally Oppenheim
— Ex Member of Parliament for Gloucester —

[signature: Sally Oppenheim]

Toffee Apple Pudding

Grate three large cooking apples on the largest gauge on the grater. Place in a shallow fireproof dish. Spread muscovado sugar thickly on top and put under a preheated grill for about 10 minutes until sugar forms a toffee coating on top of the apples.
This is economical in terms of ingredients and energy and has a delicious sweet and sour flavour. Can be served with whipped cream if family budget allows.

———————— ○ ————————

D. R. W. Wood
— Accountant, Refreshment Department, House of Commons —

DRLWood

Strawberry-Topped Pavlova

Serves 4–6
3 large egg whites
175 g (6 oz) caster sugar
½ teaspoon vanilla essence
2 level teaspoons cornflour
1 teaspoon wine vinegar
Topping
150 ml (¼ pint) double or whipping cream
225 g (½ lb) small strawberries, hulled
sugar-frosted mint leaves for decoration

Whisk egg whites until they stand in peaks; continue whisking, gradually adding the sugar, a little at a time. Fold in vanilla, cornflour and vinegar.

Draw a circle 20 cm (8 inches) in diameter on non-stick parchment paper, and pile meringue into the circle, making the sides higher than the centre.

Cook in the oven at 275–300°F/140–150°C/Gas 1–2, on the shelf below the centre, for about 1 hour. Turn off the oven and leave the pavlova inside to cool for 30 minutes. It should be crisp, tinged with brown on the surface, and soft inside.

When cold, place carefully on a serving plate and fill centre with whipped cream and top with strawberries. Decorate with sugar-frosted mint leaves and serve.

———————————— ○ ————————————

Ian Lang, MP
— Member of Parliament for Galloway and Upper Nithsdale —

Rhubarb, Rhubarb

A good nursery pudding!

Serves 4
450 g (1 lb) rhubarb, trimmed and cut into 2.5 cm (1 inch) lengths
100 g (¼ lb) brown sugar
2 eggs
300 ml (½ pint) single cream

Beat sugar, eggs and cream together and add the rhubarb.
Bake in a moderate oven at 325°F/160°C/Gas 3 for 45 minutes until set.

———————————— ○ ————————————

Rt Hon Nigel Lawson, MP
— Member of Parliament for Blaby —

SUMMER PUDDING

Serves 4–6
450 g (1 lb) raspberries
100 g (¼ lb) redcurrants
100 g (¼ lb) blackcurrants
150 g (5 oz) caster sugar
butter
day-old medium-sliced white bread, crusts cut off

In a pan, heat the fruit and the sugar very gently, just until the juices run out. Stand to cool.

Lightly butter a small china pudding basin. Line it completely with the bread, slightly overlapping the slices round the dish to form a solid lining, and making a firm base.

Fill with the fruit, using a perforated spoon and reserving quite a bit of the juice. Put a slice of bread on top and fold this over the top of the bread lining the basin.

Put a plate or saucer on top – one that fits inside the rim of the bowl – and then leave the pudding overnight with a heavy weight on top of the plate.

To turn out, go round and down the sides of the basin firmly with a palette knife. Then invert the pudding over a suitable serving dish or plate. Pour the reserved fruit juice over the pudding.

———————————— ○ ————————————

Michael Jack, MP
— MEMBER OF PARLIAMENT FOR FYLDE —

BRAMBLE MOUSSE

The only problem with this recipe is collecting the blackberries. Last time it resulted in one pair of ripped trousers, but my two small sons thought the whole exercise the next best thing to a jungle safari!

SERVES 4–6
450 g (1 lb) blackberries, cleaned
100 g (¼ lb) caster sugar
1 tablespoon powdered gelatine
2 tablespoons water
1 tablespoon lemon juice
150 ml (¼ pint) double cream
2 egg whites

Put the blackberries in a saucepan with the sugar, and simmer gently for about 15 minutes until the fruit is soft. Sprinkle the gelatine over the water and dissolve; once dissolved, stir in the lemon juice. Sieve the blackberry purée into a mixing bowl and add the gelatine mixture. Leave until the purée is beginning to set.

Whip the cream and add to the purée. Beat egg whites until stiff and add, folding carefully to combine all the purée and cream. Leave to set, then decorate with a few extra whole blackberries.

———————————————— ○ ————————————————

John L. Marshall, Member of Parliament for Hendon South, makes a similar mousse from raspberries, with the addition of 100 g (¼ lb) cream cheese, which 'gives it richness and a most pleasing texture'.

Ian Bruce, MP
— Member of Parliament for Dorset South —

Rich Chocolate Mousse

Per Person
50 g (2 oz) plain chocolate, broken into small pieces
15 g (½ oz) butter
1 egg, separated

Place the chocolate and butter in a bowl standing in a pan of hot water. Melt slowly together, then remove from heat. Cool a little, then stir in the egg yolk. Stiffly beat the egg white, and fold into the chocolate mixture. Pour into a sundae dish or wine glass and chill for 1 hour.

———————— ○ ————————

Mike Bramley
— Press Association —

Mocha Cake

Serves 4–6

100 g (¼ lb) butter
175 g (6 oz) caster sugar
3 egg yolks
4 tablespoons strong coffee

1 large packet sponge cakes
300 ml (½ pint) double cream
shelled walnut halves

Cream butter and sugar together well, then beat in egg yolks and coffee.

Slice sponge cakes laterally – three or four slices to each cake. In a 15–17.5 cm (6–7 inch) cake tin, place alternate layers of sponge and creamed mixture, starting and finishing with sponge. Cover with a saucer, top with a weight, and place in the refrigerator for at least 12 hours.

Turn out, and coat with whipped cream. Decorate with walnut halves.

———————— ○ ————————

Michael Shersby, MP

— Member of Parliament for Uxbridge —

Caramelled Grapes

These will get you out of a fix if you have little time to prepare a dinner party dessert.

Serves 4–6
900 g (2 lb) white grapes, skinned and pipped
600 ml (1 pint) double cream
225 g (½ lb) soft brown sugar

Place the grapes in a flat fireproof dish. Whip the cream and pour over the grapes. Heat the grill until red hot. Put the soft brown sugar on the cream and place under the hot grill for 2 minutes or until the sugar has caramelized.

Allow to cool and then refrigerate until required.

A variation of this dish, and an excellent stand-by, may be made with sliced bananas instead of grapes.

Gerald Howarth makes a crunchy version, using crushed digestive biscuits, bananas *and* grapes – plus a little liqueur of choice – under the cream and sugar.

———————————— ○ ————————————

Bowen Wells, MP

— Member of Parliament for Hertford and Stortford —

Rum and Bananas

This is a Caribbean recipe which I used to thoroughly enjoy when I was in the West Indies for eleven years, and which I make occasionally for my family. It is simple and quick to make – and might suit MPs in their flats in London and cause them to dream of the blue seas and skies when it has been raining here for five days solid. It might cheer them up enormously!

Serves 4–6
6 peeled bananas
butter
ground cinnamon or cloves
grated nutmeg
honey or brown sugar
juice and finely grated rind of 1 orange
1 cup dark rum
To serve
vanilla ice cream

Place the bananas in a baking dish or oven-to-table casserole and dot with butter. Sprinkle with cinnamon or cloves and a touch of nutmeg, and then pour on sufficient honey or brown sugar to cover the bananas. Sprinkle the orange rind over the top, and squeeze the juice over the bananas. Then add the cup of dark rum.

Bake in a hot oven at 400°F/200°C/Gas 6 for 15 minutes. Serve immediately with vanilla ice cream.

———————————— ○ ————————————

Nicholas R. Winterton, MP
— MEMBER OF PARLIAMENT FOR MACCLESFIELD —

Nicholas. R. Winterton

LEMON MERINGUE PIE

SERVES 4–6
1 baked pastry case, approx. 20 cm (8 inches) in diameter
1 large can sweetened condensed milk
juice and finely grated rind of 2 lemons
2 eggs, separated
2 level teaspoons cream of tartar, sieved
caster sugar

Mix together condensed milk, lemon juice and rind, egg yolks and cream of tartar. Pour this mixture into the baked pastry case.

Beat the egg whites until stiff, add 25 g (1 oz) caster sugar and beat again. Fold in another 25 g (1 oz) sugar and pile meringue on top of lemon mixture, completely covering it, and sealing it to pastry edges. Dredge with a little more sugar and bake at about 300–325°F/150–160°C/Gas 2–3 until outside is crisp but inside is still soft.

John Bowis, OBE, MP for Battersea, makes a gooseberry meringue pie. Cook 450 g (1 lb) gooseberries lightly in 50 g (2 oz) margarine until tender. Cool slightly and liquidize, with sugar to taste, 3–4 crumbled rich tea biscuits and 2 egg yolks. Cover with egg white meringue and bake as above.

———————————— ○ ————————————

J. Allan Stewart, MP
— MEMBER OF PARLIAMENT FOR EASTWOOD —

STRAWBERRY CRUNCH

This is enough for six but I guarantee there will not be any leftovers. It is a great favourite in our household. Serve with whipped cream.

125 g (4½ oz) plain flour	*FILLING*
75 g (3 oz) butter	*350 g (¾ lb) strawberries, hulled*
40 g (1½ oz) caster sugar	*3–4 tablespoons redcurrant jelly*

Put the flour, butter and sugar in food processor for 2 minutes and then press into greased round quiche dish. Chill for about 20 minutes then bake at 325°F/160°C/Gas 3 for about 30 minutes until golden brown.

When cool, wash and halve the strawberries and place on base. Heat the redcurrant jelly until dissolved, then pour over strawberries and leave until set.

———————— ○ ————————

Paul Heywood
— BANQUETING CLERK, REFRESHMENT DEPARTMENT, HOUSE OF COMMONS —

JUBILEE BLACK CHERRY PIE

SERVES ABOUT 6	*FILLING*
225 g (½ lb) plain flour	*1 large can pitted black cherries*
50 g (2 oz) lard	*50 g (2 oz) sugar*
50 g (2 oz) vegetable margarine	*1 large measure Kirsch*
½ teaspoon salt	*15 g (½ oz) cornflour*
3 tablespoons water	
1 egg, beaten	
granulated sugar	

To make the pastry, mix flour, lard and margarine together until a sandy texture is obtained. Make a well in the centre and put the salt and water in it. Mix together to form a rough dough. Roll out to the size of the top of a 15 cm (6 inch) pie dish and place in the fridge to chill for 30 minutes.

To make the filling, drain the cherries and place the juice, sugar and Kirsch in a saucepan. Allow to boil until the liquid is reduced by one-third. Dilute the cornflour in a little cold water and add to the liquid. Bring to the boil.

Place the cherries in the pie dish and cover with the hot sauce. Allow to cool.

Cover with the shortcrust pastry. Prick with a fork around the top of the pastry to make little holes. Egg wash the top of the pastry and sprinkle with granulated sugar. Bake in a preheated oven at about 350°F/180°C/Gas 4 until pastry is golden brown. Serve with whipped double cream or ice cream.

———————— ○ ————————

George Foulkes, MP
— MEMBER OF PARLIAMENT FOR CARRICK, CUMNOCK AND DOON VALLEY —

FULARSTONE TART

SERVES 4–6
75 g (3 oz) butter
75 g (3 oz) cornflour
75 g (3 oz) self-raising flour
caster sugar
2 eggs, separated
fruit of choice (preferably canned)
glacé cherries or angelica

Make the pastry first, rubbing the butter into the flours and then mixing in 4 tablespoons sugar. Add the beaten egg yolks and knead with a knife. Form into a dough, roll out and use to cover an ovenproof flat plate (Pyrex). Bake in the preheated oven at about 400°F/200°C/Gas 6 until light brown. Remove from oven and leave to cool.

When cool, cover the pastry base with the fruit of your choice (drained well if canned). Beat the egg whites until stiff, then gradually beat in about 25 g (1 oz) sugar. When the meringue is thick and glossy, fold in another 25 g (1 oz) sugar with a metal spoon. Spread this meringue over the fruit gently and evenly to cover the pie completely. Decorate with glacé cherries or angelica and bake in the oven – at the above temperature – for about 10 minutes, or until the meringue is set and golden.

○

George Gardiner, MP
— MEMBER OF PARLIAMENT FOR REIGATE —

SHADOW CABINET PUDDING

Otherwise known as 'Shambles'.

Serves 4–6
1 packet sponge cakes, broken into pieces
generous helping medium dry sherry
450 g (1 lb) meringues, broken into pieces
350 g (¾ lb) bitter (preferably cooking) chocolate, broken into pieces
300 ml (½ pint) double cream, whipped

Soak the sponge cake pieces in the sherry.

Mix sponge and sherry with the meringue and chocolate pieces, and the whipped cream – but be careful not to mash them. Refrigerate for 2 hours before serving.

(Note: Substitute any orange-flavoured liqueur for the sherry for an interesting variation, in which case a little pared zest from an orange can be added too.)

———————————— o ————————————

Viv Robins
— BBC —

Banoffi Pie

This is disgustingly sweet and bad for you but tastes delicious. The original is to be had at the Dalmeny Hotel in St Anne's, only a few miles down the road from Blackpool.

Serves 4–6
1 baked sweet pastry case
1 × 410 g (14½ oz) can condensed milk
2–3 bananas
about 150 ml (¼ pint) double or whipping cream
about 50 g (2 oz) chocolate, grated

Boil the can of condensed milk in a pan of boiling water for 3–4 hours. Leave to cool for about an hour before opening. The milk will have turned into a thick toffee.

Slice the bananas and arrange in the pastry base. Spread the toffee over the top. Cover with whipping cream and grated chocolate.

———————————— o ————————————

Chris Butler, MP
— MEMBER OF PARLIAMENT FOR WARRINGTON SOUTH —

CANADIAN CHEESECAKE

Taking about 7 minutes to prepare, less time than a Parliamentary Division, the final result is always decisively favourable.

SERVES ABOUT 6

12 digestive biscuits, crushed
50 g (2 oz) butter, melted
3 packets Philadelphia cream cheese
¾ cup caster sugar
grated rind of 1 lemon

2 teaspoons fresh lemon juice
1½ eggs, well beaten
whipped cream
mandarin orange segments
chopped walnuts

Mix crumbs with melted butter, and press into an 18.75 cm (7½ inch) flan dish.

Beat together cheese, sugar and lemon rind until soft and creamy, then mix in lemon juice and beaten egg. Bind well together. Pour into the biscuit shell, and bake at 350°F/180°C/Gas 4 for about 15 minutes or until just set, one shelf from the top of the oven. Cool before decorating with cream, mandarins and walnuts.

———————————— ○ ————————————

Dr Jeremy Bray, MP
— MEMBER OF PARLIAMENT FOR MOTHERWELL SOUTH —

Jeremy Bray

PINEAPPLE AND GINGER CHEESECAKE

A simple but delicious cheesecake, best served chilled.

SERVES ABOUT 6
50 g (2 oz) butter, melted
150 g (5 oz) digestive biscuits, crushed
FILLING
1 egg, beaten
300 g (10 oz) low-fat soft cheese (Philadelphia or St Ivel's Shape)
50 g (2 oz) sugar
TOPPING
1 can crushed pineapple, well drained, or (better) flesh of 1 small pineapple, chopped, crushed and well drained
2 cm (about ¾ inch) fresh root ginger, peeled and finely chopped
300 ml (½ pint) soured cream
50 g (2 oz) sugar

To make the biscuit base, mix the melted butter with the crushed biscuits. Press into a 22.5 cm (9 inch) flan dish or Pyrex dish, using fingers or a metal spoon.

To make the filling, whisk together the beaten egg, low-fat cheese and sugar. Spread inside the cooled case. Bake in a moderate oven at 350°F/180°C/Gas 4 until golden and lightly set, about 30 minutes.

Meanwhile, mix the crushed pineapple and chopped ginger together. Mix the soured cream and sugar in another bowl.

Remove the cheesecake from the oven and turn the oven off. Spread pineapple and ginger gently over cheesecake, then pour the sweetened soured cream over the top of that. Spread evenly and replace in the cooling oven for approximately 5 minutes (long enough to allow sugar to melt).

Remove and leave to cool. Refrigerate when cold (can be frozen).

———————— ○ ————————

Rt Hon Alfred Morris, MP

— MEMBER OF PARLIAMENT FOR MANCHESTER, WYTHENSHAWE —

A.Y. Morris.

LEMON PUDDING

This is a quick and easy, good old British pud, warming and filling, yet sharp and refreshing enough to help sustain even the frailest against a belabouring by any open-ended three-line whip. (Cambridge dieters, please avoid!)

SERVES 4–6
100 g (¼ lb) caster sugar
50 g (2 oz) soft butter
juice and finely grated rind of 1 lemon
2 eggs, separated
50 g (2 oz) self-raising flour, sifted
300 ml (½ pint) milk

Cream sugar, butter and lemon rind together. Add egg yolks to the mixture with the sifted flour. Beat well and then add milk and, finally, lemon juice. Whip egg whites until stiff and fold into the mixture.

Grease a 1.1 litre (2 pint) ovenproof dish, and pour mixture into it. Fill a roasting tin with hot water to a depth of 1.25 cm (½ inch) and stand dish in this. Place tin and contents in preheated oven at 350°F/180°C/Gas 4. Bake for 30–35 minutes until top is set and tawny brown.

———————— ○ ————————

Den Dover, MP

— MEMBER OF PARLIAMENT FOR CHORLEY —

Den Dover

CHILLED LEMON FLAN

Donated by Amanda Dover, my daughter.

SERVES 4–6
50 g (2 oz) butter
1 level tablespoon caster sugar
100 g (¼ lb) digestive biscuits, crushed
FILLING
150 ml (¼ pint) double cream
1 × 175 g (6 oz) can condensed milk
juice and finely grated rind of 2 large lemons
TOPPING
fresh lemon slices

Melt butter in a pan, add sugar then blend in the biscuit crumbs. Mix well. Turn mixture into a 17.5 cm (7 inch) pie plate or flan dish, and press into shape round base and sides of plate with the back of a spoon. Bake in a slow oven at about 300°F/150°C/Gas 2 for 8 minutes. Remove from the oven and leave to cool. Do not turn out as it will crumble.

For the filling, mix together the cream, condensed milk and lemon rind. Slowly beat in the lemon juice. Pour mixture into the flan case and chill for several hours until firm. Just before serving decorate with lemon slices in 'twists'.

———————————— ○ ————————————

Graham Bright, MP
— MEMBER OF PARLIAMENT FOR LUTON SOUTH —

MOTHER'S BREAD PUDDING

This recipe is not for the faint-hearted nor for anyone wishing to lose weight – but for politicians, I find it good for keeping one's feet firmly on the ground!

SERVES 4

Take half a loaf of bread, preferably stale, and soak it in water until wet, then squeeze it out. Add 2 eggs, 2 tablespoons shredded suet, 2 tablespoons natural brown sugar, 350 g (¾ lb) mixed dried fruit and 1½ teaspoons mixed spice. Mix all ingredients together well. Squeeze mixture into a well-greased Pyrex dish and dot top with margarine. Bake for about 1 hour at 375°F/190°C/Gas 5 until browned.

———————————— ○ ————————————

Harry Greenway, MP
— MEMBER OF PARLIAMENT FOR EALING NORTH —

NICE RICE PUDDING

Rice pudding should be eaten every day at all stages of life. For children rice pudding is body-building, for men and women of young and mature age it is sustaining and energy-giving and in old age, rice pudding gives that extra vitality which makes all the difference to life!

SERVES 4–6
butter
900 ml (1½ pints) milk
4 generous tablespoons pudding rice, washed through a sieve
3 tablespoons sugar
a pinch of salt
1 teaspoon grated nutmeg

Grease a large oval Pyrex bowl with butter. Pour in the milk and then add the well washed rice. Add sugar and salt and stir. Sprinkle with nutmeg.

Place in a preheated oven at 350°F/180°C/Gas 4 and cook for 1½ hours. Stir in the skin after 30 minutes.

Rt Hon Peter Archer, QC, MP
— Member of Parliament for Warley West —

HALF-HOUR PUDDING

A very British dish for those who can spare the half hour. It is not recommended for those trying to reduce weight.

SERVES 4
1 cup self-raising flour (or plain flour with an added teaspoon baking powder)
1 cup sultanas or small raisins
2 cups water
1 cup soft brown sugar
a large knob of butter

Mix the flour and fruit in a small pudding dish.

Pour the water into a saucepan and add sugar and butter. Warm over flame until sugar is dissolved.

Pour over mixture in the pudding dish, stir briefly and leave for a few minutes for the mixture to level off.

Bake in the oven at 375°F/190°C/Gas 5 for 30 minutes. Serve hot.

———————————— ○ ————————————

I. Gabay

— Executive Chef, Refreshment Department, House of Commons —

CABINET PUDDING

This pudding can also be made with skimmed milk and sugar substitute, and can also be served cold.

SERVES 4
4 fresh eggs
75 g (3 oz) caster sugar
600 ml (1 pint) milk
1 vanilla pod or 3 drops vanilla essence
25 g (1 oz) butter
25 g (1 oz) mixed peel
25 g (1 oz) sultanas
25 g (1 oz) glacé cherries, chopped
50 g (2 oz) plain sponge, cut into small squares
APRICOT SAUCE
4 generous tablespoons apricot jam
½ cup cold water

Beat together the eggs and sugar. Bring the milk to boiling point with the vanilla pod or essence and add (strained of pod) to the eggs and sugar. Mix well with a hand whisk or electric mixer. Pass the mixture through a fine mesh strainer.

Butter the inside of four 75 g (3 oz) caramel moulds and sprinkle with extra sugar.

Mix peel, sultanas, chopped cherries and sponge squares together and divide between the four moulds. Top up each mould with the egg mixture.

Place the moulds in a deep earthenware dish half filled with cold water and allow to cook in a preheated oven at 300°F/150°C/Gas 2 for 25 minutes or until completely set.

Meanwhile, make the apricot sauce. Boil the apricot jam and water together gently until reduced by half.

To serve, turn puddings out on to four sweet dishes, and top each one with apricot sauce.

———————————— ○ ————————————

Geoffrey Dickens, JP, MP
— Member of Parliament for Littleborough and Saddleworth —

[signature]

Norwegian Cream

This sweet is very popular amongst our dinner guests and is one my wife likes to make as the base is prepared the day before and the cream and chocolate added about an hour before dinner.

When the guests have eaten well on the first two courses and it seems unlikely that the cheeseboard will be reached, then this sweet is light, tasty and ideal.

Serves 4–6
stiff apricot jam
3 large eggs
1 level tablespoon sugar
a few drops of vanilla essence
450 ml (¾ pint) milk
4 tablespoons double cream
50 g (2 oz) plain chocolate, flaked or grated

Cover the base of a 1.1 litre (2 pint) dish with apricot jam. In a bowl fork together 2 whole eggs plus 1 extra yolk (reserving the extra white), and add the sugar and vanilla essence.

Heat the milk until hot but not boiling and pour over the eggs, stirring. Strain the custard over the jam and cover with kitchen foil. Put the dish in a roasting tin with enough water to come halfway up the sides of the dish, and cook in the oven at 325°F/160°C/Gas 3 for 1¾ hours, or until custard is set.

Lift the dish from the tin and leave to go cold.

Before serving whisk the egg white until stiff. Whip the cream until it holds its shape, and fold in the egg white. Spoon this on top of the custard to cover the pudding, and decorate with the flaked or grated chocolate.

Can also be made in individual dishes – much more convenient for a dinner party!

———————— ○ ————————

Tony Speller, MP
— MEMBER OF PARLIAMENT FOR DEVON NORTH —

Tony Speller

DEVONSHIRE JUNKET

This recipe is from Castle Hill House, Lynton.

SERVES 4–6
1.2 litres (2 pints) full cream Devonshire milk
4 tablespoons Devonshire Apple Brandy
2 level dessertspoons sugar
2 teaspoons rennet
600 ml (1 pint) Devonshire clotted cream
grated nutmeg or ground cinnamon
fresh raspberries or strawberries

Bring the milk slowly to blood heat (maximum 100°F/39°C). Remove from heat and add brandy and sugar. Stir to dissolve the sugar, then add the rennet. Pour into individual sundae dishes and leave in a warm, draught-free place, undisturbed, for 15 minutes to set. Chill.

To serve, spread surface of each dish with clotted cream, and sprinkle with nutmeg or cinnamon. Accompany with soft fruit – or whortleberries picked on Exmoor!

———————— ○ ————————

Neil Thorne, OBE, TD, MP
— MEMBER OF PARLIAMENT FOR ILFORD SOUTH —

Neil Thorne

CABINET PANCAKES

My friends, who thought that the limit of my culinary knowledge extended to boiling an electric kettle and cooking toast in a pop-up toaster, will be surprised to see me featuring in a recipe book. However, politicians can rarely resist a challenge especially when accompanied by offers of free publicity and a good deal of fattening research.

100 g (¼ lb) plain flour
25 g (1 oz) malted brown flour
¼ level teaspoon salt
1 egg, beaten
300 ml (½ pint) milk
25 g (1 oz) glacé cherries, quartered

50 g (2 oz) chopped mixed peel
25 g (1 oz) sultanas
1 tablespoon vegetable oil or lard, to fry
To Serve
brown sugar
lemon juice

Sift the flours and salt into a bowl, and make a well in the centre. Add the egg and the milk a little at a time, beating the flour into the mixture to make a smooth batter.

Add the glacé cherries, mixed peel and sultanas.

Ladle just sufficient of the batter to cover the bottom of a small frying pan, heated with the oil, and add a tablespoon of the fruit from the bottom of the mixture.

Cook until lightly brown, then toss to brown the other face. Fold edges to centre and turn over with fruit on the top. Add brown sugar and lemon juice to taste.

———— ○ ————

John Smillie
— General Manager, Refreshment Department, House of Commons —

[signature: John Smillie]

Carrie's Cloutie Dumpling

A traditional Scottish pudding, as is the writer of this recipe.

Serves about 8

1 cup sugar
1 cup breadcrumbs
1 cup shredded suet
350 g (¾ lb) raisins
225 g (½ lb) currants
1 apple, grated

450 g (1 lb) self-raising flour
1 teaspoon ground cinnamon
1 teaspoon mixed spice
1 egg
300 ml (½ pint) milk
1 teaspoon plain flour to dust cloth

Mix all the ingredients together except for the egg, milk and dusting flour, then mix in the egg and milk until a fairly stiff dough.

Scald a pudding cloth in boiling water, wring it out well, and dust with the plain flour. Place mixture on cloth and tie securely. Put into a large pot on top of a plate and cover with boiling water. Cover and boil for 3–4 hours, checking water level.

———— ○ ————

Jim Wallace, MP
— MEMBER OF PARLIAMENT FOR ORKNEY AND SHETLAND —

BOODLES FOOL

This is a very quick dessert to make.

SERVES 4–6
2 oranges
1 lemon
1–2 tablespoons caster sugar
150 ml (¼ pint) double cream
150 ml (¼ pint) single cream
½ packet trifle sponges

Grate the rind finely from 1 orange and from half the lemon. Squeeze juice from both oranges and from half the lemon. Add sugar to taste.

Lightly whip the creams together (not too thick) and stir into the fruit juice mixture.

Quarter the sponges and arrange in a dish. Spoon the cream and fruit mixture over them. (At this stage the pudding will appear runny but it thickens after being chilled.) Serve with macaroon biscuits.

———————————— ○ ————————————

Rt Hon Malcolm Rifkind, QC, MP
— MEMBER OF PARLIAMENT FOR EDINBURGH, PENTLANDS —

CHOCOLATE AND CHESTNUT DESSERT

This is a very rich dessert, so serve small portions with a biscuit. The quantities given are sufficient for twelve people.

100 g (¼ lb) fresh butter
100 g (¼ lb) caster sugar
225 g (½ lb) plain chocolate, chopped or grated
3 tablespoons liquid (equal parts rum and water, or rum and strong coffee)
a few drops of vanilla essence
1 can chestnut purée
DECORATION
whipped cream or 50 g (2 oz) melted chocolate
toasted shredded almonds

Cream softened butter, then add caster sugar and beat well together.

Put chopped or grated chocolate into a bowl with the rum liquid and place over steam from pan of water, until liquid. Stir in the vanilla essence.

Meanwhile, turn the chestnut purée out of the can and beat with a fork until smooth. Stir the chestnut purée into the butter and sugar until quite smooth, then add the melted chocolate, one-third at a time, until all ingredients are evenly blended. Pour into a prepared tin (as below) and smooth level.

Have ready an oblong loaf tin which has been oiled, and place a double band of greaseproof paper at the bottom with the ends coming above the edges of the tin, for easy lifting. Leave the tin in the refrigerator until contents have set firmly.

When required, turn on to a serving dish and coat with whipped cream (or melted chocolate) and sprinkle with shredded and toasted almonds. If liked, the whipped cream can be served separately.

———————— ○ ————————

Sir Carol Mather, MC
— Ex Member of Parliament for Esher —

MISTERTON MOUSSE

Serves 4
100 g (¼ lb) butter
100 g (¼ lb) brown sugar
4 tablespoons coffee essence
100 g (¼ lb) brown breadcrumbs
Decoration
whipped cream
toasted chopped almonds

Beat butter and sugar together. Heat coffee essence and pour over breadcrumbs. Mix all together. Pour in a mould to set.

When ready, turn out on to a serving dish and decorate with whipped cream and toasted chopped almonds. This is delicious with sliced oranges.

———————— ○ ————————

Andrew Bowden, MBE, MP
— Member of Parliament for Brighton Kemptown —

LEMON MOUSSE

Serves 4–6
4 large eggs
175 g (6 oz) caster sugar
grated rind of 1 lemon
juice of 2 large lemons
150 ml (¼ pint) water
15 g (½ oz) powdered gelatine

Separate the eggs, cracking the yolks into one basin and the whites into a second, larger basin. Add the sugar to the yolks along with the grated lemon rind and lemon juice. To get the right lemon flavour in this recipe, you need about 3–4 tablespoons lemon juice. Using a wooden spoon, stir the egg yolk mixture well to blend all the ingredients thoroughly.

Measure the water into a saucepan and sprinkle in the gelatine. Allow to stand for a few minutes, then place over low heat and stir until the gelatine has dissolved. Do not boil. Draw the pan off the heat then, holding it well above the mixing basin, add the gelatine to the lemon mixture, pouring in a thin, steady stream. Stir well all the time to blend the gelatine into the mixture evenly. Allow the mixture to stand until it begins to thicken and set. It should not take longer than 30 minutes.

Stiffly beat the egg whites and, using a metal spoon, fold into the lemon mixture. Pour into a serving dish and chill for several hours until firm. Serve with cream.

Barry Sheerman, MP
— MEMBER OF PARLIAMENT FOR HUDDERSFIELD —

PENNINE CHOCOLATE SURPRISE

SERVES 6
125 g (4½ oz) butter
125 g (4½ oz) caster sugar
150 ml (¼ pint) milk
2 egg yolks
250 g (9 oz) Menier chocolate broken into pieces
about 25 almond macaroons, approx. 3.75 cm (1½ inches) in diameter
brandy

Soften the butter, and cream with the sugar until soft. Set to one side.

Scald the milk and when cool beat in the egg yolks.

Melt the chocolate in a bowl over hot water and when completely melted stir in the milk and egg yolk mixture. Add this to the creamed butter and sugar and beat until smooth.

Oil a charlotte mould or soufflé dish. Dip the macaroons in the brandy and, beginning and ending with macaroons, layer the macaroons and chocolate mixture in the dish. Leave to stand for 2 hours and then freeze for 24 hours. Remove from freezer 1 hour before serving.

Doug Hoyle, MP
— MEMBER OF PARLIAMENT FOR WARRINGTON NORTH —

Doug Hoyle

SYLLABUB WITH CARAMELIZED GRAPES

Although delicious it is fattening and if taken very often one could end up like a pelican:
'A wonderful bird is the pelican
His beak will hold more than his belican.
He can take in his beak
Food enough for a week
But I'm damned if I know how the helican!'

SERVES 4
juice and finely grated rind of 1 lemon
75 g (3 oz) caster sugar
2 tablespoons brandy
2 tablespoons sherry
300 ml (½ pint) double cream
CARAMELIZED GRAPES
75 g (3 oz) granulated sugar
2 tablespoons water
seedless grapes

Soak the grated lemon rind and the juice with the caster sugar, brandy and sherry for 2–3 hours.

Meanwhile, prepare the caramelized grapes. Place the granulated sugar with the water in a thick-bottomed saucepan. Boil steadily until it caramelizes. Turn off the heat and dip grapes (held by the stem with tweezers) into the mixture. Coat each grape and remove quickly from syrup and stand to drain on greaseproof paper. These will take half an hour to harden but should be eaten fairly promptly or they go sticky.

To finish the syllabub, whip the double cream and add to the lemon and alcohol mixture, blending evenly. Serve chilled with the caramelized grapes.

———————————— ○ ————————————

Neil Hamilton, MP
— MEMBER OF PARLIAMENT FOR TATTON —

GINGER ICE CREAM

There is so much talk about diets nowadays that, although my wife watches my calories very closely indeed, left to my own devices, I would follow the Mark Twain maxim – 'eat what you like and let the food fight it out inside you'! This ice cream – and the pâté on page 20 – are two of my favourites which I hope you will enjoy.

SERVES 4–6
125 ml (4 fl. oz) water
75 g (3 oz) granulated sugar
3 egg yolks
300 ml (½ pint) double cream
75 g (3 oz) preserved stem ginger, finely chopped
brandy snaps or ginger biscuits, broken (optional)

Place the water and sugar in a pan and heat gently, stirring until dissolved. Increase the heat and boil steadily until the syrup reaches a temperature of 225°F/110°C; at this stage a little of the cooled syrup will form a thread when drawn between the thumb and forefinger.

Cool slightly, then pour on to the egg yolks, whisking until the mixture is thick and mousse-like.

Whip the cream until it stands in soft peaks, then fold in the ginger. Fold into the egg mixture. To make it *extra* delicious, you can add at this stage bits of brandy snap broken up or small pieces of ginger biscuit.

Turn into a rigid freezerproof container, cover, seal and freeze until firm.

Transfer to the refrigerator 20 minutes before serving to soften.

Robert Banks, MP
— Member of Parliament for Harrogate —

Snow Queen

Serves 4
300 ml (½ pint) double cream
2 tablespoons brandy
1 tablespoon caster sugar
100 g (¼ lb) meringue, roughly broken

Whisk the cream until stiff and stir in the brandy and caster sugar. Fold in the roughly broken meringue. Taste and add more sugar – and brandy! – if necessary. Pour the mixture into a 600 ml (1 pint) pudding basin or bombe mould.

Cover, seal and freeze.

To serve, unwrap, unmould, place on a serving dish and thaw for 15 minutes in the refrigerator. Decorate with raspberries, strawberries or glacé cherries, or serve with melba sauce.

David Knox, MP
— Member of Parliament for Staffordshire, Moorlands —

Honeydew Ice Cream

On the first occasion I canvassed, I was accompanied by an elderly choleric ex-military gentleman. He thundered on the first door like the Secret Police. There was no reply within ten seconds and he repeated the performance. A timorous middle-aged lady came to the door and he barked, 'How are you going to vote – Conservative, Liberal or Labour – and make it snappy!'

Serves 4–6
1 large Honeydew melon
4 egg yolks
75 g (3 oz) caster sugar
600 ml (1 pint) double cream
2 tablespoons Cointreau or peach brandy
2 egg whites, stiffly beaten

Scoop out the flesh from the melon and cut into tiny dice.

Beat the egg yolks with the sugar until very creamy. Heat the cream to just below boiling point and then pour it on the egg yolks in a thin stream, stirring all the time. Cook over a gentle heat, taking care not to let it boil, until the mixture thickens. Add the Cointreau or peach brandy and cool a little before stirring in the diced melon.

Fold in the stiffly beaten egg whites and freeze for 6 hours. Transfer the ice cream to the fridge 30 minutes before you serve it, to soften it slightly.

———————— ◯ ————————

Rt Hon David Howell, MP
— MEMBER OF PARLIAMENT FOR GUILDFORD —

BANANA ICE CREAM

Here is quite a good recipe for using the contents of all those banana skins, which seem to be so plentiful around the place.

Serves 4–6
3–4 bananas, depending on size (the riper the better)
2 eggs, separated
300 ml (½ pint) double or whipping cream
a little icing sugar

Liquidize bananas and egg yolks together.

Whip egg whites and add to mixture.

Whip cream and add to mixture.

Add icing sugar to taste.

Then freeze. If for a party, this can be frozen directly in a freezer-proof glass bowl.

———————— ◯ ————————

Cakes, Biscuits and Breads

Mrs Edwina Currie, MP
— MEMBER OF PARLIAMENT FOR DERBYSHIRE SOUTH —

Edwina Currie

CARROT CAKE

This is from a book of recipes presented to me by the Notre Dame School in Sheffield.

SERVES 10
2 eggs, separated
200 g (½ lb) soft brown sugar
150 g (6 oz) Kraft Vitalite Sunflower Margarine, melted
2 tablespoons warm water
125 g (5 oz) wholemeal flour
1 teaspoon baking powder
½ teaspoon mixed spice
a pinch of salt
25 g (1 oz) walnuts, chopped
25 g (1 oz) sultanas
150 g (6 oz) carrots, peeled and grated
ICING
100 g (¼ lb) Kraft Philadelphia Soft Cheese
100 g (¼ lb) icing sugar, sieved
grated zest of ½ lemon

Preheat oven to 375°F/190°C/Gas 5. Grease and line the base of a 17.5 cm (7 inch) cake tin or 900 g (2 lb) loaf tin.

Cream together the egg yolks, sugar, margarine and water. Sieve the dry ingredients into a bowl, add the nuts, sultanas and carrots, and mix well. Make a well in the centre and add the egg mixture. Stir well and mix.

Whisk the egg whites to soft peaks. Fold carefully into the cake mixture.

Pour into the prepared tin and bake in the preheated oven for 45–50 minutes, until a skewer inserted in the centre comes out clean. Cool on a wire rack.

To make the icing, cream together the cheese and icing sugar until soft and creamy, then add the grated lemon zest. Swirl over the cake, and decorate with a little extra finely grated lemon or orange zest.

The cake can also be baked in a microwave. Bake in a 900 g (2 lb) loaf-shaped container suitable for the microwave for 10 minutes. Leave to stand for 5 minutes before turning out on to a cooling rack. When cold top with the icing.

The cake will freeze for up to 6 months. (*267 calories per serving.*)

———————————— ○ ————————————

Mark McLaren
— RESEARCH ASSISTANT TO ANDREW ROWE, MEMBER OF PARLIAMENT FOR KENT MID —

WESTMINSTER APPLE CAKE

Delicious just as cake, but is especially good served with ice cream as a dessert, either hot or cold.

100 g (¼ lb) butter
225 g (½ lb) self-raising flour
100 g (¼ lb) sugar
2 eggs
milk if necessary
225 g (½ lb) cooking apples, peeled, cored and diced
75 g (3 oz) dried fruit
juice of 1 lemon
a pinch of salt
1 teaspoon ground cinnamon

Rub the butter into the flour until the texture is like breadcrumbs. Add the sugar and eggs. Mix to a moist consistency, perhaps adding a drop of milk to help. Mix in the apple dice and the dried fruit, plus the lemon juice, salt and cinnamon. Stir all the ingredients well together.

Place the mixture in a round greased or greaseproof-paper-lined baking tin, and bake in a preheated oven at 300°F/150°C/Gas 2 for 1½ hours.

———————————— ○ ————————————

Peter Viggers, MP
— MEMBER OF PARLIAMENT FOR GOSPORT —

FRESH BLACKCURRANT CAKE

Fresh raspberries may also be used for this cake.

100 g (¼ lb) butter or margarine
100 g (¼ lb) caster sugar
2 standard eggs
175 g (6 oz) self-raising flour
2 tablespoons milk
100 g (¼ lb) blackcurrants, washed, stalked and dried

Cream butter and sugar together until fluffy, then beat in the eggs, one at a time, a spoonful of flour with each egg. Sieve remaining flour and fold into mixture along with the milk. Finally fold in the blackcurrants.

Pour into a 20 cm (8 inch) sandwich tin and bake in the preheated oven at 350°F/180°C/Gas 4 for 40 minutes.

———————————— ○ ————————————

Rt Hon John Biffen, MP
— Member of Parliament for Shropshire North —

John Biffen

Muesli Cake

Food that needs junk verse
Foretells something worse.

225 g (½ lb) plain flour
175 g (6 oz) margarine
100 g (¼ lb) muesli
175 g (6 oz) brown sugar
350 g (¾ lb) chopped dates and mixed dried fruit
3 eggs, beaten
75 ml (2½ fl. oz) milk

Rub the flour and margarine together until the texture is like breadcrumbs. Add the muesli, sugar, dates and dried fruit and mix well.

Mix the beaten eggs and milk in well, and then put into two small loaf tins or one 20 cm (8 inch) round cake tin.

Bake in the preheated oven at 300°F/150°C/Gas 2 – the loaf tins for 1 hour, the larger one for a bit longer.

———————————— ○ ————————————

Richard Livsey, MP
— MEMBER OF PARLIAMENT FOR BRECON AND RADNOR —

BARA BRITH (Moist Fruit Cake)

50 g (2 oz) butter
200 g (7 oz) sugar
100 g (¼ lb) sultanas
50 g (2 oz) walnuts, chopped
50 g (2 oz) glacé cherries, chopped
1 teaspoon bicarbonate of soda
1 cup water
1 egg, beaten
300 g (10 oz) self-raising flour

Put the butter, sugar, sultanas, walnuts, cherries, bicarbonate of soda and water into a pan and boil for 3 minutes. Leave to cool.

Add egg and flour and mix well.

Place in a greased and lined loaf tin and bake in a preheated oven at 350°F/180°C/ Gas 4 for 1½ hours.

———————— ○ ————————

John Watson
— EX MEMBER OF PARLIAMENT FOR SKIPTON AND RIPON —

YORKSHIRE CHRISTMAS CAKE

This cake is recommended for those who have difficulty in keeping to a diet. Its effect, upwards, upon both waistline and scales will be sufficient to restore any lost determination.

FILLS A 19 CM (7½ INCH) TIN

250 g (9 oz) brown sugar	350 g (¾ lb) sultanas
250 g (9 oz) butter	350 g (¾ lb) currants
5 small eggs	75 g (3 oz) raisins
350 g (¾ lb) plain flour, sieved	75 g (3 oz) almonds, chopped
1 tablespoon dark treacle	50 g (2 oz) glacé cherries
a pinch of salt	50 g (2 oz) candied peel
¼ teaspoon mixed spice	1 glass brandy

Beat the sugar and butter together. Add each egg separately and beat. Add the flour a little at a time, until all the ingredients are mixed well. Stir in the dark treacle and the dry ingredients, followed by the dried fruit etc. Stir well and pour in the brandy last of all. Mix well.

Put in a tin lined with greaseproof paper. Wrap a layer of newspaper around the tin and secure with string. (This prevents the cake from burning or going hard on the outside.)

Bake in the preheated oven at 275°F/140°C/Gas 1 for 3½ hours (very moist) or 4 hours (firm). Cool.

Cover with almond paste made with 350 g (¾ lb) ground almonds, 175 g (6 oz) each of icing and caster sugars, lemon juice, almond essence and 1 egg. Ice with a royal icing made with 450 g (1 lb) icing sugar and 2 egg whites.

———————————— ○ ————————————

Jerry Hayes, MP
— MEMBER OF PARLIAMENT FOR HARLOW —

AMAZING CAKE

No added fat, no added sugar, no eggs, high fibre – amazingly healthy! For the perfect politician – not too sickly but keeps the bowels moving and waist trim. So fibrous, the ideal curtailment for tedious tea-time conversations.

CONSTITUENTS
225 g (½ lb) dates
300 ml (½ pint) warm water
175 g (6 oz) wholewheat flour
50 g (2 oz) ground almonds
3 teaspoons baking powder
1 tablespoon carob powder (optional)
1 teaspoon ground mixed spice
450 g (1 lb) mixed dried fruit
grated zest of 1 lemon or orange
4 tablespoons orange juice
TOPPING
flaked almonds

Construction Policy

Chop dates and soften in the warm water.

Mix together all the dry ingredients, including the fruit, then add the zest, dates, their water and the orange juice. Stir well.

Spoon into a greased 900 g (2 lb) loaf tin lined with greaseproof paper, smooth the surface, and top with flaked almonds. Bake at 325°F/160°C/Gas 3 for 1½ hours.

Leave to cool for a few minutes then remove from tin and leave to get cold on a cake rack.

Miss Janet Fookes, MP
— Member of Parliament for Plymouth, Drake —

Janet Fookes

Fruit Cake

I once used this recipe (borrowed from my mother) to provide a prize in a Conservative Party raffle. I have never discovered whether the winner survived. The Chairman of the Catering Committee certainly has, despite receiving at Christmas each year this fruit cake enveloped in marzipan and chocolate icing!

The dried fruit content of the cake can be varied to taste.

450 g (1 lb) sultanas
175 g (6 oz) large raisins, chopped
2 tablespoons sherry or brandy
225 g (½ lb) butter
225 g (½ lb) caster sugar
5 eggs, beaten well
100 g (¼ lb) self-raising flour, sifted
100 g (¼ lb) plain flour, sifted
225 g (½ lb) ground almonds, sifted
175 g (6 oz) mixed peel
225 g (½ lb) glacé cherries, halved
1 dessertspoon lemon curd or honey

Put the dried fruit in a basin, add the alcohol, cover and leave overnight.

Cream the butter and sugar together until light and fluffy, then add the eggs a little at a time, beating well after each addition. Lightly fold in the sifted flours and ground almonds, alternating with the soaked dried fruit, peel, cherries and lemon curd or honey, until evenly distributed. Do not beat.

Grease and flour a 20–30 cm (10–12 inch) cake tin, and pour in the cake mixture. Cover with a piece of good greaseproof paper and place in the oven preheated to 325°F/160°C/Gas 3. Bake for 30 minutes then reduce oven temperature to 300°F/150°C/Gas 2. Bake for another 2½ hours, then remove paper and continue baking cake for a further 30 minutes approximately. Cool in the tin for a while, then turn out on to a cake rack and leave to become completely cold.

———————— ○ ————————

Albert McQuarrie
— Ex Member of Parliament for Banff and Buchan —

HAPPINESS CAKE

Especially good for Members of Parliament.

TAKE:
1 heaped portion of true love
1 heaped cup of perfect trust and confidence
1 heaped cup of tenderness (the most tender available)
1 heaped cup of good humour
1 tablespoon of good spirits (the more spirited the better)
BLEND WELL WITH:
1 heaped cup of unselfishness
a dash of interest in all one does, and
1 good helping of work

Mix all the ingredients with a pint of sympathy and understanding combined. Flavour with loving companionship. Bake well all your life. Ice with kisses, fond hope and tender words.

This cake keeps well, and should be served often.

———————— o ————————

Christopher Jones
— BBC —

PAT STANSFIELD'S BOILED CAKE

Pat Stansfield is the lady who organizes the BBC's radio and television studios at Westminster – and calms the nerves (and powders the noses) of fractious politicians before they face the microphones and the cameras.

150 g (5 oz) butter
150 g (5 oz) dark brown sugar
450 g (1 lb) mixed cake fruit

1 cup milk
2 eggs, beaten
225 g (½ lb) self-raising flour, sifted

Place butter, sugar, fruit and milk in a large saucepan and heat gently until butter has melted. Mix all well together. Allow to cool slightly, then add the beaten eggs and mix well. Add sifted flour and mix. Place in a greased and lined 20 cm (8 inch) cake tin, and bake for about 2 hours at 300°F/150°C/Gas 2. Allow to cool in tin. Wrap in foil and keep for at least 3 days before eating.

If well wrapped in foil, this cake keeps many weeks, and makes an excellent Christmas or birthday cake. If liked, a level teaspoon of mixed spice; or a level teaspoon of finely grated orange rind; or 100 g (¼ lb) glacé cherries; or 50 g (2 oz) of chopped walnuts (or any combination of the above) may be added.

———————————— ○ ————————————

Dr Keith Hampson, MP
— MEMBER OF PARLIAMENT FOR LEEDS NORTH WEST —

CHOCOLATE CAKE

1 tablespoon cocoa powder mixed to a paste
with 2 tablespoons boiling water
100 g (¼ lb) soft margarine
100 g (¼ lb) caster sugar
100 g (¼ lb) self-raising flour
2 eggs

CHOCOLATE ICING
2 tablespoons water
50 g (2 oz) butter
50 g (2 oz) caster sugar
75 g (3 oz) icing sugar
25 g (1 oz) cocoa powder

Put all the cake ingredients in the Magimix and process for 10 seconds. Scrape down bowl and process for another 5 seconds. Divide between two equal-sized tins and bake in the preheated oven at 350°F/180°C/Gas 4 for 20 minutes. Turn out of the tins and cool.

To make the icing, place water, butter, and caster sugar in a small saucepan and bring to the boil. Measure the icing sugar and cocoa powder into the Magimix and process for 1 second to mix. Add the boiling mixture from the saucepan and process until mixed.

Use to ice the cakes.

———————————— ○ ————————————

John Wheeler, MP
— MEMBER OF PARLIAMENT FOR WESTMINSTER NORTH —

SACHER TORTE

My recipe is especially popular with my women's committee and goes down well after a good claret!

FILLS A 15 CM (6 INCH) CAKE TIN
50 g (2 oz) butter
75 g (3 oz) sugar
100 g (¼ lb) plain chocolate, melted
2 large eggs, separated
40 g (1½ oz) ground almonds (or other nuts)
2 level tablespoons self-raising flour
FILLING
apricot jam
TOPPING
50 g (2 oz) plain chocolate
50 g (2 oz) butter

Line cake tin with good greaseproof paper.

Cream the butter and sugar together and then add the cooled melted chocolate. Beat well to amalgamate and then beat in the egg yolks. Fold in the almonds and flour very lightly.

Beat the egg whites well, and slowly and lightly fold them into the cake mixture.

Pour into the prepared cake tin and bake in a preheated oven at 350–375°F/180–190°C/Gas 4–5 for 30–45 minutes or until top begins to crack slightly (it will rise up and then sink on cooling).

Cool completely and then cut in half horizontally. Add jam filling. Cover with the melted chocolate and butter mixture.

It is a *very* rich, moist cake. It keeps well in an airtight tin, and can also be frozen, un-iced.

Rt Hon Neil Kinnock, MP
— MEMBER OF PARLIAMENT FOR ISLWYN —

Neil Kinnock

WELSH CAKES

Traditionally a heavy griddle is used to cook these Welsh cakes, but a good solid frying pan will do. Serve them as they are or buttered, with good Welsh honey.

100 g (¼ lb) butter or margarine
225 g (½ lb) self-raising flour
75 g (3 oz) currants
75 g (3 oz) caster sugar
1 large egg, beaten
milk, if necessary

Rub the butter into the flour until the mixture resembles breadcrumbs, then add the currants and the sugar.

Add the egg to the mixture and use your hands to mix to a dough. Add a little milk if it is a little too dry.

Now roll the dough out on a floured working surface. Roll it to about 6 mm (¼ inch) thick and cut it into rounds with a 6.25 cm (2½ inch) cutter.

Heat the griddle or frying pan over a medium heat and cook the cakes for about 2–3 minutes on each side. Make sure they are cooked through and a good golden brown colour.

———————————— ○ ————————————

George Park
— Ex Member of Parliament for Coventry North East —

George Park

ABBEY BISCUITS

75 g (3 oz) butter
1 tablespoon syrup
1 tablespoon water
1 cup self-raising flour
1 cup Quaker Oats
¾ cup sugar
1 cup desiccated coconut
1 teaspoon bicarbonate of soda

Put the butter, syrup and water into a pan and melt over a low heat. Mix the remaining ingredients well together, then mix in the contents of the pan. Roll into walnut-sized balls (damp hands help), and space out on to greased or greaseproof-paper-lined baking trays. Bake in the preheated oven at 375°F/190°C/Gas 5 for approximately 10–15 minutes. The addition of ½ teaspoon ground ginger makes a nice variation.

———————————— ○ ————————————

Simon Burns, MP
— Member of Parliament for Chelmsford —

CHELMSFORD BARS

Break up a large packet of digestive biscuits. Pour into 225 g (½ lb) melted butter. Press into the bottom of square dish or baking tin. Sprinkle on top 100 g (¼ lb) chopped walnuts, 2 small packets plain chocolate chips, and a half packet desiccated coconut. Pour over 1 large and 1 small can of condensed milk.
Bake until golden brown at 350°F/180°C/Gas 4. Cool, then cut into squares.

———————————— ○ ————————————

Dr Rhodes Boyson, MP
— MEMBER OF PARLIAMENT FOR BRENT NORTH —

Rhode Boyson

DR RHODES BOYSON'S SPECIALLY RECOMMENDED LANCASHIRE OAT BISCUITS

My recipe is a traditional one from the Lancashire hill farms. Oats was the only cereal that could generally be ripened there and it was the base for porridge, speedy pudding – warmed-up porridge – and oat cakes and biscuits.

100 g (¼ lb) self-raising flour
a pinch of salt
75 g (3 oz) Quaker Oats
25 g (1 oz) caster sugar
75 g (3 oz) fat (a mixture of butter, margarine and lard is ideal)
1 tablespoon milk

Mix together the flour, salt, Quaker Oats and sugar. Rub in the fats and mix to a stiff paste with the milk.

Roll out thinly on a floured board and cut into rounds.

Bake on a greased baking sheet in a moderate oven (350°F/180°C/Gas 4) for about 15–20 minutes.

———————————— ○ ————————————

Kenneth Warren, MP
— MEMBER OF PARLIAMENT FOR HASTINGS AND RYE —

STICKY GINGERBREAD

This recipe has been proved as excellent canvassing sustenance at General Elections – but when confronted by floating voters, Honourable Members should not shake hands!

1 cup milk
1 cup black treacle
1 cup demerara sugar
50 g (2 oz) margarine
50 g (2 oz) lard
1 teaspoon bicarbonate of soda
1 egg, beaten
3 cups plain flour
1 teaspoon each ground ginger, mixed spice and cinnamon
some chopped preserved ginger, if available

Put the first six ingredients in a pan and heat to melt the fats and treacle. Cool slightly, then add the beaten egg.

Add all the remaining ingredients and beat well. Pour into a lined tin and bake in a slow oven at about 275–300°F/140–150°C/Gas 1–2 for 2 hours.

———————————— ○ ————————————

Rt Hon Robert Sheldon, MP
— MEMBER OF PARLIAMENT FOR ASHTON-UNDER-LYNE —

SCONES

MAKES 12
225 g (½ lb) plain flour
4 teaspoons baking powder
a little salt
75 g (3 oz) butter
50 g (2 oz) caster sugar
1 egg

Mix flour, baking powder and salt with the butter to a breadcrumb consistency. Add sugar, then egg. Mix well. Roll out to about 2 cm (¾ inch) thickness and cut in small rounds.

Space out on a baking sheet and bake in a hot oven preheated to 425°F/220°C/Gas 7 for 10 minutes.

Eat and enjoy with lightly whipped cream and home-made strawberry conserve.

———————————— ○ ————————————

Neville Trotter, FCA, JP, MP
— MEMBER OF PARLIAMENT FOR TYNEMOUTH —

TYNEMOUTH TEA BREAD

1 teacup mixed fruit
1 teacup brown sugar
1 teacup water
50 g (2 oz) butter or margarine
1 dessertspoon marmalade if wished
225 g (½ lb) self-raising flour
1 level teaspoon bicarbonate of soda
1 level teaspoon mixed spice if liked
1 egg, beaten

Put fruit, sugar, water, butter and marmalade (if used) in a saucepan and melt together until the sugar dissolves. Leave to cool, and then tip in the flour, bicarbonate and spice (if used), and add the beaten egg. It makes a very runny mixture.

Grease and line a 900 g (2 lb) loaf tin, pour in the mixture, and bake for about 1 hour in an oven preheated to 350°F/180°C/Gas 4.

Instructions for eating: cut into slices and spread with butter.

———————————— ○ ————————————

Lewis Carter-Jones
— EX MEMBER OF PARLIAMENT FOR ECCLES —

YORKSHIRE SPICE LOAVES

This particular recipe has been followed by my wife's family for longer than we can remember! It is an old hand-down. We find it a useful stand-by which will keep for 3–4 weeks without deterioration.

After a vote on the guillotine, let them eat cake!

900 g (2 lb) self-raising flour
1 teaspoon ground mixed cake spice
a good pinch of salt
225 g (½ lb) margarine, in pieces
225 g (½ lb) caster sugar
225 g (½ lb) dark brown sugar
450 g (1 lb) currants
225 g (½ lb) seedless raisins
600 ml (1 pint) milk (fresh or powdered, I always use powdered)
3 medium eggs, beaten
2 teaspoons lemon juice or PLJ
2 tablespoons rum or brandy

Sift the flour into a large mixing bowl, and add the mixed spice together with a little salt. Rub the fat into the flour, then add the sugars and dried fruit and stir well until it is all thoroughly mixed.

Stir in the milk, beaten eggs, lemon juice and rum or brandy until the mixture is well mixed and quite soft – add a little more milk if necessary.

Grease four 450 g (1 lb) loaf tins and divide the mixture between them. Place in the centre of a preheated oven at 350°F/180°C/Gas 4 for about an hour. Test by piercing with a skewer: if it comes out clean, the loaves are ready.

Store loaves in an airtight tin. They are best kept for at least 1 day before eating, and they keep moist for 3–4 weeks. Serve sliced and spread with a little butter or margarine.

———————————— ○ ————————————

Sir Victor Le Fanu
— Serjeant at Arms —

Victor Le Fanu

Four Moist Granary Loaves

I am fortunate enough to be married to a master baker, so here is a recipe for four moist granary loaves. I think we should encourage a revival of home baking, as the products taste so much better, and it is a cheaper process than buying bread, scones, croissants etc from the shops.

40 g (1½ oz) fresh yeast
approx. 750 ml (1¼ pints) tepid water
1 kg (2½ lb) granary flour
20 g (¾ oz) salt
50 g (2 oz) fat (vegetable oil, lard or butter)
100 g (¼ lb) black treacle
1 teaspoon caraway seeds

Dissolve the yeast in the bulk of the tepid water, holding back about 75 ml (2½ fl. oz). A hand whisk is useful for this.

Put the flour, salt, fat and treacle in the mixer and pour the yeast liquid in on top. Using the dough hook, mix at medium speed until a soft pliable dough is obtained, using the reserved water – or more – if necessary. (The dough can also be mixed by hand. Combine fat, flour and salt in a bowl and add the treacle to the yeast and water mixture. Pour liquid on to dry ingredients and mix well before kneading dough for 5–10 minutes.)

Leave dough in a large bowl, covered with a cloth, for 40 minutes in a warm place.

Take out dough, sprinkle with caraway seeds, and knead them into the dough. Return to covered bowl and warm place for a further 20 minutes.

Cut into four equal parts, and form each into a bun-shaped loaf. Grease two baking trays, and put two loaves on each tray (to allow for rising). Cover each tray with a cloth and leave in a warm place for about 45 minutes or until, when slightly pressed by thumb, the risen loaves spring back into shape. (If your oven is too small for all four loaves, set one tray of loaves in a cool place, and the other in a warm place and cook the latter first.)

Put the trays in the upper half of the oven preheated to 425–450°F/220–230°C/Gas 7–8, and bake for 20 minutes. Reduce the temperature to 375°F/190°C/Gas 5 and cook for a further 15 minutes. Test the bottom of a loaf for a hollow ringing sound, then remove and slide on to cake racks until cooled.

Cyril D. Townsend, MP
— MEMBER OF PARLIAMENT FOR BEXLEYHEATH —

Cyril D Townsend

THE STAFF OF LIFE

What could be simpler than a loaf of new bread? What could be more wholesome and welcoming to a tired Westminster man or woman after a week of rich feeding? Here is an absolutely foolproof recipe for the Staff of Life.

Empty about two-thirds of a bag of flour (about 900 g or 2 lb) into a big bowl. Rub in about 50 g (2 oz) margarine and a large pinch of salt. Make a well in the centre.

Activate a packet of dried yeast according to instructions on the packet; or with a dessertspoon of sugar to 50 g (2 oz) live yeast in 600 ml (1 pint) warm water in a warm place for as long as it takes to make a good frothy head of yeast.

Pour the warm water with yeast (you may need more warm water if you're using a heavy flour) into the well in the centre of the flour and knead hard for at least 10 minutes on a firm flat floured board. This will leave you feeling at peace with the world!

Put the lump of dough back in the basin covered with a damp cloth somewhere warm (but not hot – don't cook it) for the dough to rise and double in size. This normally takes about an hour, depending on how warm a place you have. Then knead it again, divide in four and put in four oiled, greased and floured 450 g (1 lb) loaf tins to rise a second time.

At this stage (before putting in tins) roll the loaves in cracked wheat or sesame seeds to give the crust a special bite.

After the second rising the loaves should be risen just above the sides of the tins. Cook in a hot falling oven at 450°F/230°C/Gas 8 (reducing heat after first 15 minutes to about 375°F/190°C/Gas 5) for 35–40 minutes, or until the loaves sound hollow when their bases are tapped.

Turn them out on to a wire rack to cool. Your kitchen will smell delicious and all your friends and family will be happy and hungry and waiting for tea! PS: If you want to keep any for tomorrow, hide it until it is cool enough to freeze.

Note: New dry yeasts need only one proving. Experiment with different flours and mixtures of flours.

———————————— ○ ————————————

CONFECTIONERY AND PRESERVES

Mrs Ann Winterton, MP
— MEMBER OF PARLIAMENT FOR CONGLETON —

Ann Winterton.

MARMALADE

Seville oranges can be frozen whole in 1.8 kg (4 lb) batches and removed to make marmalade throughout the year. A grapefruit and/or a whole lemon can be added to Seville oranges to vary the flavour.

2.75 kg (6 lb) sugar
1.8 kg (4 lb) Seville oranges
2 litres (3½ pints) water
juice of 1 lemon

Put sugar and sufficient jam jars in a cool oven to warm through.

Wash oranges and place *whole* in preserving pan with the water. Bring to the boil, cover and simmer for 2 hours. Remove from heat, drain fruit out of the liquid and cut it into quarters when cool enough to handle. Scrape pulp from skin with knife and drain this, juice and pips in a sieve over the preserving pan. Cut orange peel into strips to required thickness and return to pan.

Return pan to heat, add warmed sugar and lemon juice, and stir until setting point is reached – approximately 15–20 minutes. To test for set, place a little marmalade on a cold saucer, return to refrigerator and a 'skin' should form after a minute or so.

Remove marmalade from heat and leave to cool for 10–15 minutes. Stir well to distribute peel and pour into clean warm jam jars. Top with waxed discs and screw-tops of jars.

———————————— ○ ————————————

Michael Shersby, MP
— MEMBER OF PARLIAMENT FOR UXBRIDGE —

MARROW AND APPLE CHUTNEY

There was a young lady from Harrow
With a penchant for apple and marrow
Said a green grocer from Putney
You must make some good chutney
And buy the fruit and the veg from my barrow.

MAKES ABOUT 3–3.6 KG (7–8 LB)
1.8 kg (4 lb) marrow
75 g (3 oz) salt
900 g (2 lb) cooking apples, peeled, cored and finely chopped
450 g (1 lb) shallots, peeled and finely chopped
25 g (1 oz) bruised peppercorns, chillies and ginger, tied in a muslin bag
450 g (1 lb) soft brown sugar
1.8 litres (3 pints) vinegar

Peel the marrow and chop into small pieces. Layer the pieces in a basin with the salt and leave overnight. Drain well.

Place apple and shallot in the preserving pan with the marrow and spices and cook gently until tender. Add the sugar and vinegar and cook until the mixture thickens to the consistency of jam. Remove the bag of spices, put the chutney into warm jars and cover with greaseproof paper. Seal with waxed cloth or plastic.

———————————— ○ ————————————

Dame Jill Knight, DBE, MP
— MEMBER OF PARLIAMENT FOR BIRMINGHAM, EDGBASTON —

I can thoroughly recommend these two recipes. The Tomato Jam is very unusual but delicious, and the Marrow Lemon Cheese is an excellent way of using marrows when the garden produces too many and one has become tired of them as a vegetable.

TOMATO JAM

3.1 kg (7 lb) large ripe tomatoes
6 lemons
3.6 kg (8 lb) sugar
600 ml (1 pint) water

Blanch and skin tomatoes, cut in half, and place in a large pan. Remove rinds, white pith and pips from lemons and slice fruit thinly. Add to tomatoes with the sugar and water. Bring to the boil and then reduce heat until mixture is simmering gently. When the jam 'jellies' on a cold plate, put into jars and cover. Store in a cool place.

MARROW LEMON CHEESE

1.8 kg (4 lb) marrow, weighed after marrow is cut and peeled
1.35 kg (3 lb) sugar
juice and finely grated rind of 6 lemons
225 g (½ lb) butter

Cook prepared pieces of marrow until soft, then drain well. Liquidize or mash well with a fork. Return to the pan and add the sugar, lemon juice and grated rind and the butter. Cook all to a cream – about 20 minutes. Put in pots and cover, and serve as Lemon Cheese.

Roy Hughes, MP
— MEMBER OF PARLIAMENT FOR NEWPORT EAST —

TOFFEE

This toffee recipe must be 100 years old and has been a great favourite in the family over the years. Whatever the activity – housework, gardening, driving, holidaying, or driving up the motorway! – the toffee adds its own special zest.

225 g (½ lb) sugar
50 g (2 oz) butter (not margarine)
2 tablespoons golden syrup
5 tablespoons cold water
1 teaspoon vinegar

Boil the ingredients together for 15–20 minutes, stirring frequently. The mixture will thicken and darken in colour when ready. To test, pour a few drops into a cup of cold water. It should harden instantly.

Turn out into a heatproof dish or tin and allow to cool. Break into pieces gently with a small hammer.

○

Roger Gale, MP
— MEMBER OF PARLIAMENT FOR NORTH THANET —

ALLIANCE FUDGE

A smooth, bland and anodyne confection that will appeal to all – briefly! More-ish at first but sickly and cloying upon over-indulgence. The home-made variety is the best; the professional product usually relies heavily on packaging and the contents tend to be disappointing.

1 can evaporated milk
900 g (2 lb) granulated sugar
50 g (2 oz) real butter
4 dessertspoons cocoa powder (or several drops of vanilla essence or other flavouring)

Put all ingredients into a strong saucepan and bring mixture to the boil, stirring *all the time*. Do not allow mixture to boil until all the sugar has melted completely. Boil for about 15–20 minutes, stirring *constantly*.

Once the mixture has reached 'soft ball' stage – at a temperature of about 235–245°F/113–118°C, or when syrup dropped into cold water forms a soft ball which flattens on removal from water – take off heat. Beat vigorously until it begins to stiffen slightly. Pour into a greased or wax-paper-lined square tin. Cut with a sharp knife before it sets fully.

———————————— ○ ————————————

RECIPE INDEX

NAME INDEX